"Through Jesus, Christians have a 'G[...] so prone to allowing circumstances, tr[...] aches, and worries to cloud the sun o[...] book radiates hope, shining with the[...] 'Surely there is a future, and your hope will not be cut off' (Prov. 23:18). I initially read *A Bright Tomorrow* because I was asked to do so in view of possibly writing an endorsement. Now that I've written it, I intend to read the book again because it encouraged me so much the first time."

Donald S. Whitney, Professor of Biblical Spirituality and Associate Dean at the Southern Baptist Theological Seminary, Louisville, KY; author of *Spiritual Disciplines for the Christian Life*, *Praying the Bible*, and *Family Worship*

"I interact with a lot of people who have faced the devastation of losing a child. When your worst fears have become your reality, some wrestling with whether or not you can genuinely trust God moving forward and what that should look like is inevitable. I've wanted a book that I could give to people who ask me what to do with the very real fears they have about the future. And now I have it. *A Bright Tomorrow* offers readers a sound, scripture-saturated, concise, and winsome invitation to trust God with everything."

Nancy Guthrie, Author of *Hearing Jesus Speak Into Your Sorrow*

"This isn't pastoral hyperbole—I absolutely love Jared Mellinger's new book, *A Bright Tomorrow*. As those in union with Christ, we are hard-wired for hope, whether or not we have yet to see, experience, and enjoy this wiring and hope. God will bring to completion the good work he has begun, not only in us as his beloved daughters and sons, but also in his entire creation. This is our hope. This is our living, heart-transforming, all-creation renewing, mission-engaging hope. With art and heart, Jared not only throws the curtains wide open on the glories of our all-things-new future, he also demonstrates the present power of remembering God's future into our present moment."

Scotty Ward Smith, Pastor Emeritus, Christ Community Church, Franklin, TN; Teacher in Residence, West End Community Church, Nashville, TN

"This book will help you to see. When your yesterday or today has been bleak, the road ahead looks only dark. Jared has brought together much of what Scripture says about tomorrow in a way that you will have courage to forge ahead with hope. Read it slowly."

Ed Welch, Bestselling author; faculty member at CCEF

"I am grateful for Jared's book and Aggie's story where 'Grace Reigns' even where shadows fall and the sorrows rain. Such profound confidence in the past, present and future promises of God that cannot fail is gospel triumph."

Bryan Chapell, Senior Pastor, Grace Presbyterian Church

"This is a beautiful book torn out of a father's own anguished heart. Reading these words it was clear, 'not only is it important to Jared that his readers hear this and believe it, but it is most important to the writer himself.' We all have fears about the future and sometimes those fears can be acute, even paralyzing. Reading Jared's book was soothing medicine that helped set my mind on things that are unseen but real and enduring. Give this book to someone you care about who is anxious about the future."

Rankin Wilbourne, Pastor of Pacific Crossroads Church, Los Angeles, CA; author of *Union with Christ*

"We live in a scary world. Fear of an unseen, menacing future often troubles our hearts and robs us of joy. Jared Mellinger's *A Bright Tomorrow* demonstrates from God's Word that everyone who trusts Jesus has a Protector who is almighty, always faithful, overwhelmingly loving, and ever present. And Pastor Mellinger speaks from experience: for their own family, the Mellingers are embracing the hope that comes from God's rock-solid promises."

Dennis E. Johnson, Professor of Practical Theology, Westminster Seminary California

"We occupy a time where fear is the dominant chord: fear the future, fear death, fear pain. Mellinger's book abounds in practical and biblical wisdom pointing us to the bright future we have in Christ. God has promised us an inheritance, goodness, mercy, and resurrected life. This is a timely word and a book that needs a wide reading. Christians can be eternal optimists because we already know the end of the story."

Patrick Schreiner, Professor of New Testament at Western Seminary

A Bright Tomorrow

How to Face the Future Without Fear

Jared Mellinger

New
Growth
Press

WWW.NEWGROWTHPRESS.COM

New Growth Press, Greensboro, NC 27404
www.newgrowthpress.com
Copyright © 2018 by Jared Mellinger

Cover Design: Faceout Studios, faceoutstudio.com
Interior Typesetting and E-book: Lisa Parnell, lparnell.com

ISBN 978-1-948130-01-1 (print)
ISBN 978-1-948130-52-3 (e-book)

Library of Congress Cataloging-in-Publication Data on File

Printed in the United States of America

25 24 23 22 21 20 19 18   1 2 3 4 5

Contents

Introduction

THE FUTURE OF every Christian is incredibly bright, and the way to live a fruitful life in the present is to embrace all that God has spoken about that bright future. We are like travelers, whose view of the path ahead profoundly shapes our experience of life's journey. When our thoughts of the future are ill-informed or full of doubt, it drains our joy and peace. But when our thoughts are biblically informed and full of faith, we flourish.

I've written this book to help those of us who are troubled by the days to come. The future is dark at times, and courage does not come naturally for any of us. Changes are daunting, uncertainties are frightening, old age and death are concerning.

And yet, 2 Thessalonians 2:16–17 says that God our Father has loved us and given us eternal comfort and good hope through grace. You are so greatly loved by the Father, and he is so generous in his grace, that *eternal comfort* and *good hope* have been secured for you.

The goal of this book is to push back fear and unbelief and to awaken our souls to the boundless comfort and hope we have in Jesus Christ.

At the same time, this book is not just for those who look to the future and are troubled. It is also for those who don't tend to think much about the future. Even those who are not given to over-concern about the days to come need to discover the blessings that come to us as we live in the good of our future in Christ.

All Christians need to think rightly about the future. Christ sustains us, satisfies us, and changes us by the power of a forward-looking hope.

The main idea driving this book is that the best way to counter future-oriented fear is to remember what God promises regarding our future. The problem for most of us is that we spend more time dwelling on the things we *don't* know about our future than the things we *do* know about it. We must learn to remember our future as God has revealed it in his Word. The things we know about the days to come ought to shape the way we view the things we don't know.

This Is Your Future

What do we know about the days to come? We know that God gives more grace (James 4:8). For every changing circumstance you face, there will be new mercy from the unchanging God of grace. His mercies never come to an end; they are new every morning (Lamentations 3:22–23). That includes your day tomorrow.

We know that our good Father has given us great and precious promises (2 Peter 1:4), and not one word of all the good promises the Lord has made to us has ever failed (Joshua 21:45). We go through life leaning (even collapsing, when we have no strength) on the promises of God.

We know that goodness and mercy shall follow us all the days of our lives, and that nothing can separate us from the love of God in Christ Jesus. He will hold you fast and no one will snatch you from his hand.

We know that in Christ, the future has invaded the present. The Bible uses the language of *firstfruits* to signify that the single end-time harvest has begun. The resurrection of Christ from the dead is the beginning of the great harvest that includes our resurrection (1 Corinthians 15:20–23). When Christ rose from the dead and ascended into heaven, we who are united to Christ were raised up with him and seated with him in the heavenly places (Ephesians 2:6). Now our lives are hidden with him, and we eagerly await the day when Christ appears and we appear with him in glory (Colossians 3:3–4).

We know that whatever trials we face, God will be with us to guide and preserve us. "When you pass through the waters, I will be with you; and through the rivers, they shall not overwhelm you; when you walk through fire you shall not be burned, and the flame shall not consume you" (Isaiah 43:2).

We know that all our days are in the sovereign hand of a good and mighty God. Even when we forget our bright future, he does not. "For I know the plans I have for you, declares the LORD, plans for welfare and not for evil, to give you a future and a hope" (Jeremiah 29:11). We can be confident about the future, not because we know everything the future holds, but because we know the One who holds it.

We know that the day is coming, and will soon be here, when we together will hear the loud voice of the One seated on the throne, declaring that the dwelling place of God is with man and that he is making all things new (Revelation 21:3–5).

Encountering the God of Hope

It's true that some biblical reminders of the future function as warnings and wake-up calls for Christians: "The end of all things is at hand; therefore be self-controlled and sober-minded" (1 Peter 4:7); "Let us keep awake and be sober" (1 Thessalonians 5:6); "Therefore, stay awake, for you do not know on what day your Lord is coming" (Matthew 24:42).

But that is not Scripture's dominant theme regarding our future in Christ. Biblical reminders about the future aim more at comfort and courage than they do at caution or correction. The message of "Be ready!" is loud, but the message of "Be full of hope!" is even louder.

Our future is more glorious than we know. This bright future is what we discover and apply throughout this book.

Chapter 1 explores the difficulty of facing the future with confidence. In chapter 2 we look at how Jesus helps us overcome the fear of the future. The following chapters present the key biblical categories that equip us to face the future: future grace (chapter 3), hope (chapter 4), and the promises of God (chapter 5). Chapter 6 celebrates the security we have in knowing that nothing can separate us from God's love.

The second half of the book connects the confidence we have in Christ to specific areas of life: future trials (chapter 7), parental fears (chapter 8), cultural decline (chapter 9), aging (chapter 10), and dying (chapter 11). Chapter 12 concludes with our ultimate hope that the Lord Jesus Christ will make all things new.

Because of the indestructible confidence we have in Christ, we are learning, by the grace of God, to face the future without fear and to anticipate a bright tomorrow. As Christians, we rest in the truth that there is no better future imaginable than the future that has already been secured for us in the gospel of grace. And God has given us his Spirit and his Word to reveal the riches of this future to us.

Eternal comfort? It's yours. Good hope? Yours.

My prayer for you is captured in Romans 15:13: "May the God of hope" use this book to "fill you with all joy and peace in believing, so that by the power of the Holy Spirit you may abound in hope."

Chapter 1

A Bright Tomorrow

The difficulty of facing the future with confidence

THERE WAS A day in the autumn of 2008 when my wife, Meghan, walked into our bedroom with a smile and handed a few index cards to me. She had drawn pictures on them in a style that intentionally mimicked the art of a five-year-old. We've learned that there is a lot of joy and beauty to be found in childish-looking art, so sometimes we create our own.

The first index card said "A new job!" at the top, and had a picture of a stickman preaching behind a pulpit. The stickman, I gathered, was me. I had been a pastoral intern at Covenant Fellowship Church in Glen Mills, Pennsylvania, and, after leading the singles ministry for a short time, I was asked to be the senior pastor. I was twenty-eight years old, which meant there wasn't anything especially *senior* about me other than the title. Yet in just a few months I would be stepping into a ministry position that involved leading a staff of experienced pastors and a church that was larger than what I was most familiar with. It was exciting. And daunting.

No matter what job you have, stepping into a new role or facing a difficult task tends to raise questions about the future: *What if I fail or burn out? What if I am ineffective? What if the company falls apart or I am laid off? When will I transition out of this role, and what will that be like? What if this responsibility crushes me in the meantime?*

Martyn Lloyd-Jones has a chapter on fear of the future in his book *Spiritual Depression*. He says that when the future dominates and oppresses us, it is often because we know the importance of our assignment and we know our own weakness and inadequacy for the task.[1]

Days of Blessing

The next index card Meghan gave me said "A new home!" at the top. There was a drawing of the house we would soon be moving into, which in this particular rendering happened to look exactly like every other home a child would draw, complete with enormous flowers the size of people and a sun shining from a corner of the sky.

At the time, we were a family of five, living in a small two-bedroom townhome in West Chester, Pennsylvania. We were one of the only growing families in those townhomes. Meghan and I slept in one bedroom, our two boys slept in the other bedroom, and our little girl slept in a Pack 'n Play that barely fit in our small bathroom. I remember neighbors looking at us with amusement as our family piled in and out of our minivan in what always felt to me like an elaborate circus act.

The new job had allowed us to buy our first home, and we found a place near the church. A new home is a great blessing, and yet buying a home usually involves wrestling with a number of questions about the future: *How secure is our income? Will God provide for us? How steady is the economy? What if the house is structurally unsound and collapses on us? What if our experience is like that old Tom Hanks movie,* The Money Pit, *where they buy a house that looks good but the plumbing is messed up, the stairs collapse, the electrical system goes up in flames, and the bathtub falls through the floor?*

The final index card is where I learned the most exciting news: "A new baby!" On the card, Meghan had drawn a picture of a family with four kids. In addition to the other changes in life, we now had the indescribable joy of another child joining the family.

Children have a unique way of bringing our anxieties about the future to the surface: *Will our child be healthy and develop normally? Will my mistakes as a parent ruin my children? Will he or she walk with the Lord? What kind of world will my children grow up in, given the moral challenges and political changes our culture is facing?*

We stood together in our room that day, knowing that we were in the middle of a happy whirlwind of change. An unknown future was teeming with excitement, blessings, uncertainties, and challenges.

Meghan gave me a hug and kissed me. It was one of those vivid moments in life, recorded in my memory on vintage home video, with Daniel Stern's voice from *The Wonder Years* narrating the moment.

That autumn of 2008 was a time of blessing for me, and the road ahead was bright.

When Trials Come

When I first started writing about looking to the days ahead with courage and the good news of our future in Christ, I hadn't faced any severe trials in life. I was most familiar with the challenges that "happy changes" can bring.

But then, shortly after I began writing, our family faced the greatest trial we have known when our two-year-old daughter, the youngest of our six kids, was diagnosed with cancer.

That experience changed me, and it has inevitably shaped this book.

The summer of 2016 marked ten years of service for me as a pastor. That June, I began a sabbatical. I spent the first few days of the sabbatical studying for this book. The introduction and the chapter summaries had been completed, the publisher approved my proposal, and I was eager to use the first part of my sabbatical to study the believer's future in Christ and why all Christians should face the future with confidence.

I spent one day studying the promises of God. I spent another day studying the return of Christ and the resurrection of the body. I spent a full day studying Romans 8.

During that week, we noticed that our daughter was having health challenges. Her name is Agatha; we call her Aggie. Aggie's breathing was labored, and she had several swollen lymph nodes on her neck and one on the side of her chest.

The next morning, I was planning on traveling with my wife, Meghan. The two of us were getting away to a beach house for a few days, to reflect on and celebrate the previous ten years of life and ministry. We decided late Saturday night to take Aggie to the hospital, just to make sure that everything was okay.

I called Marty Machowski, who is a good friend, fellow pastor, talented author, and my small group leader. For your kids, Marty writes books; for my kids, he writes books *and* does emergency babysitting. When Marty arrived to watch our kids, Meghan and I left for the hospital with Aggie.

I threw in my bag the two books I had been reading that day. (Some people go places without taking books with them, but that seems to me to be a terrible way to live.) One was a valuable book called *Rejoicing in Lament: Wrestling with Incurable Cancer and Life in Christ*, by Todd Billings, who at the age of thirty-nine was diagnosed with a rare form of incurable cancer. I was learning from him the role of lament in the Christian life, and how to face the future with confidence amid severe suffering.

The other was a great little book by Ray Ortlund on Romans 8, called *Supernatural Living for Natural People*. One of the things I had read in that book is this sentence:

A strong confidence in God's loving intentions and enveloping care fortifies us to face whatever life throws at us.[2]

Little did I know what life would throw at me that same day.

Only a few hours after I'd read that sentence, we were in the hospital with Aggie. They laid her on her back and she was unable to breathe. They immediately transferred her to the PICU (Pediatric Intensive Care Unit), where they provide the highest level of care for sick children.

It was a long night with no sleep and many tears, as we prayed for Aggie's life to be preserved. We were shocked and heartbroken when they told us that Aggie has a type of cancer called T-cell lymphoblastic lymphoma. For the next three weeks, Meghan and I lived in the hospital. Currently, Aggie continues on a two-year treatment plan with chemotherapy and regular hospital appointments.

This book is not an autobiography, but I have written it in the midst of a very personal fight to face my own future with confidence. I often fall short of the hope and courage I ought to have as a Christian. I've written down in these chapters the truths I need to be reminded of again and again.

Yet I Will Be Confident

Whatever our circumstances, God has promised that we have an ever-present help in time of need (Hebrews 4:16). Left to ourselves, our hearts would be ruled by fear. But God has not given us a spirit of fear. He gives us, as the hymn "Great Is Thy Faithfulness" says, "strength for today and bright hope for tomorrow."

Jesus Christ empowers us to face the future with confidence.

In Psalm 27:3, the psalmist declares, "Though an army encamp against me, my heart shall not fear; though war arise against me, *yet I will be confident*" (italics mine).

When we look to the future, we see armies encamped against us. We see our own sin, we see a world opposed to God, we see creation groaning under the effects of the fall, and we see the Devil himself stalking us. We hear the sounds of war. And we feel weak. We know that sickness, difficulties, and death await us. We question our spiritual strength and doubt our security. The future seems to spiral out of control.

In these moments, Christ comes to us and helps us lift our weary heads. *"Yet I will be confident."* This is the Christian's battle cry: *Yet I will be confident!* "Strengthen the weak hands, and make firm the feeble knees. Say to those who have an anxious heart, 'Be strong; fear not!'" (Isaiah 35:3–4).

The reason for our confidence is given in Psalm 27:1: "The LORD is my light and my salvation; whom shall I fear? The LORD is the stronghold of my life; of whom shall I be afraid?"

You are not without light in the darkness.

You are not without hope.

Christ is the stronghold of your life.

As our stronghold, Christ does not come to make our lives easy but to defend us against fear. Our fretful anticipation of trouble is often more troubling than the trouble itself. Therefore, our need is not so much to be delivered from the presence of trials as it is to be delivered from our fears of the future.

Godly Optimism

Those who are in Christ have every reason to be optimistic about the future. Hope dominates our outlook. We laugh at the days to come. We look at everything that could possibly come our way in life and consider ourselves more than conquerors.

The Bible promotes optimism, but it is a certain kind of optimism. Ours is not the secular optimism of positive thinking, but the godly optimism of Christian hope. This optimism is marked by realism and mixed with grief. We are sorrowful yet always rejoicing (2 Corinthians 6:10). We know that in this world we will have trouble, but we take heart to know the One who has overcome the world (John 16:33). Weeping may last for the night, but joy comes with the morning (Psalm 30:5).

Natural optimism is simply a matter of temperament, and is neither a virtue nor a requirement for the Christian. The temperamental optimist does not have an advantage over the temperamental pessimist in the Christian life or in the exercise of Christian hope. True hope thrives in the darkness. It is through tears of lament that we see the beauty of our hope most clearly.

This book presents the message of Christian optimism, with the voice of confidence in Christ, grounded in his finished work in the past and in the promise of future grace.

Randy Alcorn says, "Because of the certainty of Christ's atoning sacrifice and his promises, biblical realism is optimism."[3]

At church, we have recently been singing a hymn by Mary Bowley Peters called "All Will Be Well." It has been a great encouragement as I seek to look ahead with confidence.

> We expect a bright tomorrow,
> all will be well.
> Faith can sing through days of sorrow,
> "All is well."
> On our Father's love relying,
> Jesus every need supplying,
> In our living, in our dying,
> all must be well.[4]

Yes, in light of the character and promises of God in Christ, all *must* be well! The bright tomorrow is coming! Our future is better than we can comprehend. Tomorrow is bursting with joy.

Tomorrow Is a Happy Thing

Cornelis Venema, in his excellent book, *The Promise of the Future*, reassures Christians:

> The future does not loom darkly on the horizon as something to be feared. It is something eagerly expected and anticipated, something which the believer is convinced is bright with the promise of the completion and perfection of God's saving work.[5]

Likewise, Charles Spurgeon says,

> A Christian can look forward to tomorrow with joy. Tomorrow is a happy thing. It is one stage nearer glory, one step nearer heaven, one more mile sailed across life's dangerous sea, one mile closer to home. Tomorrow is a fresh lamp of the fulfilled promise that God has placed in His firmament. Use it as a guiding star or as a light to cheer your path. Tomorrow the Christian may rejoice. You may say that today is black, but I say that tomorrow is coming. You will mount on its wings and flee. You will leave sorrow behind. Be of good cheer, fellow Christian, tomorrow can have nothing negative for you.[6]

Tomorrow is a happy thing. You don't know everything about your future, but you know the most important parts.

- God will be with you.
- Christ will pray for you.
- The Holy Spirit will empower you.
- God will supply all your needs.
- The Lord will protect you.
- The love of God will keep you.
- All things will work for your good.
- The defeat of sin and death is sure.
- You will see Christ face to face.
- You will worship the Lamb who was slain.
- Your body will be resurrected.
- Your sorrows will be no more.
- You will be with loved ones in Christ.
- You will be richly rewarded.
- Christ will make all things new.

We can't let this biblical vision of the future grow blurry.

I have this problem in life where sometimes my glasses get terribly dirty and I don't even know it. Then, after a few weeks, I remember to clean my glasses, or I clean them because someone tells me they can barely see my eyes. Suddenly the whole world is new. Everything is clear.

That's what hope is like. Hope wipes away the cloudiness of our fears and gives us a clear outlook on changing circumstances, present sorrows, parenting challenges, aging, cultural decline, politics, economic uncertainty, death, and the future of all things.

As we embrace our future in Christ, it shapes our lives and our character in the present.

I need this book as much as anyone. I want to grow in being able to look to the future with an unflinching boldness. And I want to help other Christians experience this joy-filled hope as well.

How do we face the future with confidence in Christ? It starts by hearing Jesus speak to our fears.

Questions for Reflection

1. Read Psalm 27. What are some of the truths that helped the psalmist face the future without fear?

2. What does fear of the future look like in your life? Take time to pray that God would embolden you and deliver you from fear of the future.

Chapter 2

Jesus Speaks to Our Fears

We overcome fear of the future
by remembering our future in Christ

THE EVENING BEFORE Jesus died, he spoke words of great importance to his disciples. He knew the long-awaited hour had arrived. He knew the evil betrayal he must face, the agonizing death he must die, the fierce wrath he must endure. And he knew that the hearts of his disciples were heavy regarding the future.

Chapters 13–17 of the Gospel of John record the words Jesus spoke that night. He told his disciples that he was returning to the Father. He explained that he was departing and would no longer be with them. Not only that, he told them that they would remain in a world in which they would be hated. He said that they would be kicked out of synagogues and even put to death.

So much for a feel-good pep talk! What kind of a coach tells his team that they are going to be slaughtered?

As the disciples considered their future, they were fearful, distressed, and lonely.

Are we going to make it? How can we face the future? If Jesus really cared about us, why would he leave us?

We tend to think that the severity of our anxiety is abnormal, and anxiety gains momentum through that lie. But this passage in John is a reminder that we are not alone in having troubled hearts and fearful minds. Our anxious predictions and negative forethoughts are common to humankind.

"Let Not Your Hearts Be Troubled"

The disciples of Jesus occupied a unique place in salvation history. They were about to witness the Son of God as he went to the cross and ascended to heaven's throne. And yet they were not concerned about Jesus that night; they thought only of themselves. Jesus said to his disciples, "Now I am going to him who sent me, and none of you asks me, 'Where are you going?'" (John 16:5).

Anxiety tends to produce self-absorption. The fear of the future will distract us, consume us, enslave us, and rob us of comfort and courage. The stronger our anxiety, the weaker our communion with God becomes, and the more vulnerable we are to Satan's attacks. "In quietness and in trust shall be your strength" (Isaiah 30:15), but our fretting about the future weakens and exhausts us.

We sometimes think that worry will help us discover solutions and control the future, but it won't. Worry has never prepared anyone for anything. You cannot control the future through anxiety. Worry is a thief of joy; it is a liar and a sellout. Worry promises preparation but leads to panic.

Jesus knows the concerns of his people. He rescues us from our fears because he cares for us. This is the testimony of the redeemed: "I sought the LORD, and he answered me and delivered me from all my fears" (Psalm 34:4). Our own lives have often evidenced God's power to deliver from fear.

On that night before he was crucified, Jesus said, "Let not your hearts be troubled, neither let them be afraid" (John 14:27). Here is the Son of God, moments away from bearing the sins of the world, yet he comforts others! This amazes me every time

I consider it. On his way to the cross, he speaks to our fears. He draws near to us. He cares for us like no one else and loves his disciples to the end.

Consider the life and character of the One who tells us not to be troubled. We have a Savior who experienced all that we fear: he experienced the poverty of having nowhere to lay his head (Matthew 8:20); he shed tears of anguish as he wept by the tomb of Lazarus (John 11:35); people rejected him and were offended by him (Luke 4:28–29); he was slandered and many bore false witness against him (Mark 14:56); he knew the betrayal of a man who claimed to be a friend (Matthew 26:15); and he was unjustly tried, mocked, beaten, and crucified (Mark 15:16–37).

Yet Jesus always looked to the future trusting the Father's good purposes. In John 17, he anticipates his crucifixion and exaltation with a sense of triumph as he prays to his Father. Luke 9:51 says that he set his face to go to Jerusalem, fulfilling Isaiah's prophecy of a Servant who would set his face like a flint. Hebrews 12:2 says that Jesus endured the cross for the joy that was set before him. He humbled himself and became obedient to death in anticipation of the day when every knee would bow and every tongue confess that Jesus Christ is Lord (Philippians 2:8–11).

Christ is our forerunner. We are united to him. And it is because he faced his future, and because he has secured our future and sovereignly reigns over the future, that we can face whatever lies ahead.

Who is best equipped to speak to your fears? Without a doubt, it is the Lord Jesus Christ. "For we do not have a high priest who is unable to sympathize with our weaknesses, but who in every respect has been tempted as we are, yet without sin" (Hebrews 4:15).

The Tenderness of Christ

Jesus speaks to our anxieties about the future in Luke 12. In verses 4–8 he says,

> "I tell you, my friends, do not fear those who kill the body, and after that have nothing more that they can do. But I will warn you whom to fear: fear him who, after he has killed, has authority to cast into hell. Yes, I tell you, fear him! Are not five sparrows sold for two pennies? And not one of them is forgotten before God. Why, even the hairs of your head are all numbered. Fear not; you are of more value than many sparrows. And I tell you, everyone who acknowledges me before men, the Son of Man also will acknowledge before the angels of God."

This is much different from the way we are accustomed to addressing fear of the future in ourselves and in others.

Jesus does not tell us to be more like the natural optimist. Worriers should not envy the apathetic. It is not uncommon in a marriage to have one person more inclined to anxiety and the other more inclined to "faith." But often what passes as faith is natural optimism. What looks like steadiness is sometimes aloofness. You might wish that you could be more laid-back in your temperament, but that is not the answer. To be more laid-back would likely mean that you become less responsible, less aware, less involved.

Also, note that Jesus is not dismissive of our fears. He doesn't insult us. He doesn't say, "Stop worrying like an idiot." He doesn't give us commands to stop fearing without also giving us weapons in the fight against fear. He listens to us. He reasons with us. He is compassionate, he calls us his friends, and he corrects sinful fears gently. "You are more valued than many sparrows," he says.

The strength of our daily anxieties along with our blurry vision of the future is often discouraging. But we must remember that the presence of anxiety does not mean that we are without faith. Those who are in Christ need to know that our faith defines us more deeply than our anxieties. God has not forgotten you; he is the one sustaining your faith in him.

Jesus also shows the limits of the things we fear in this life. Don't freak out over those who kill the body, he says, "and after that have nothing more that they can do." Rather, he says, fear the One who has authority over your eternal destination. In other words, we should compare the future things we tend to worry about with the one thing truly deserving our worry: divine judgment in hell.

This is not an attempt to scare us; it is intended to fill us with courage and comfort. Ultimately, Jesus' main point is not, "It could be worse." He is saying that it absolutely will be better. Jesus reminds us of the eternal hell we have been spared in order to renew our hope in him.

Have you stopped to consider what your future would be without Christ? Fear gains the upper hand when we forget the future we deserve. We must never forget that Jesus decisively dealt with the one thing we should truly be worried about. Romans 5:8 says that while we were still sinners, Christ died for us. "Since, therefore, we have now been justified by his blood, much more shall we be saved by him from the wrath of God" (Romans 5:9).

The future is terrible for those who are not in Christ. It will be "the punishment of eternal destruction" (2 Thessalonians 1:9). Unrepentant sinners "will drink the wine of God's wrath, poured full strength into the cup of his anger" (Revelation 14:10).

But the glory of the gospel, as John Stott puts it, is that "Divine love triumphed over divine wrath by divine self-sacrifice."[1]

You are not saved by your own bravery or resourcefulness, or by any good deeds you have done, but because you acknowledge the Lord Jesus Christ. This wrath-free future is not secured by your worry-free life, but by Jesus' sin-free life and substitutionary death. By removing the fear of judgment and hell, Christ makes us invincible. The day is coming when the Son of Man will acknowledge you before the angels of God (Luke 12:8). Christ our advocate will speak our names. And far from it being a day of regret and shame, we will be presented blameless and with great joy (Jude 24).

From Fear to Faith

Notice the way that Jesus leads us from fear to faith. It's not that we are to stop thinking about the future. Rather, *we overcome fear of the future by remembering our future in Christ.* This simple truth has far-reaching implications for our lives. If we are presently overcome with fear and anxiety regarding our future, it is because we have lost sight of our true future in Christ.

What does Jesus tell his weak disciples in John 13–17 when confidence is waning, fear is rising, and they are troubled about the future?

A Place Prepared

In John 14, Jesus reminds them that he is going to prepare a place for them: "And if I go and prepare a place for you, I will come again and will take you to myself, that where I am you may be also" (14:3).

This is the truth that Anne Bradstreet used to fight her fear of the future when her house was destroyed by fire. Anne was a mother of eight children who lived among the Pilgrim settlers in Massachusetts. In the midst of grief and loss, she found the strength to praise God with a contented heart by remembering her future home.

> And when I could no longer look,
> I blest his Name that gave and took,
> That laid my goods now in the dust . . .

Then comes the forward look:

Thou hast an house on high erect
Fram'd by that mighty Architect,
With glory richly furnished,
Stands permanent tho' this be fled.[2]

Jesus reminds us that he is the Mighty Architect. He has gone to build a house on high and is preparing a permanent and richly furnished place for you. He will return to take us there, when heaven and earth are joined as one.

The Presence of the Spirit

Jesus also promises in John 14:16 that his work on earth has not come to an end, but is carried on through another helper. "And I will ask the Father, and he will give you another Helper, to be with you forever." This means that:

- The peace Jesus gives will be experienced through the Spirit.
- The obedience Jesus requires will be empowered by the Spirit.
- The truth Jesus taught will be illuminated by the Spirit.
- The witness Jesus calls us to, even through opposition, will be emboldened by the Spirit.

We see these same disciples full of the Spirit in the book of Acts. They are invincible and courageous, praising God with holy joy and performing many signs and wonders. They defy earthly powers and declare that they cannot but speak of what they have seen and heard as witnesses of Christ (Acts 4:20). When they are imprisoned and beaten, they rejoice that they are counted worthy to suffer dishonor for the name of Jesus (Acts 5:41).

What explains this spiritual power? They had been given another Helper, the Holy Spirit, to be with them forever. The Spirit affirmed their unshakable future in Christ.

The Promise of Life

In John 14:19, Jesus then gives his disciples the promise of future life: "Because I live, you also will live." Here is the hope of victory over death through our union with Christ. His death and resurrection would vanquish death and secure eternal life for his people.

Christian, you will rise to life just as surely as Christ rose on the third day. This is your future in Christ. Pessimism, panic, despair, and worry will give way to a bright tomorrow.

In John 17, Jesus, our Great High Priest, then prays for his followers regarding their future. He reminds his disciples of his ultimate desire for us and the future he has secured for us as he prays out loud: "Father, I desire that they also, whom you have given me, may be with me where I am, to see my glory that you have given me because you loved me before the foundation of the world" (John 17:24).

One day we will no longer experience difficulties and temptations in relation to the future. It is not until we leave this world that we will experience full freedom from fear. But Jesus has not left us without the truths needed to resist fear and grow in hope.

The God Who Delights to Bless You

In Luke 12, Jesus speaks to our fear that harm will befall us, and our fears related to money, provision, and material possessions. Then he says in Luke 12:32, "Fear not, little flock, for it is your Father's good pleasure to give you the kingdom."

This is how Jesus speaks to our anxieties about the future. The command ("Fear not") is followed by compassion ("little flock") and comfort ("It is your Father's good pleasure to give you the kingdom"). The phrase "good pleasure" is telling us something about the heart of the Father toward us, and this is precisely what our fears of the future are inclined to disbelieve. Do you believe that God delights to bless you? He is not a miserly ruler, a cold-hearted king, or a stingy man like Ebenezer Scrooge.

This verse reminds us of who God is, and who we are in relation to him. If we are a little flock, he is our Shepherd. If he is our Father, we are his children. If he gives us the kingdom, he is our King. In Christ, the Creator of the universe is our Shepherd, Father, and King.

Our Shepherd. We are called sheep ("little flock") because we belong to God, and because God wants us to look to him for guidance, provision, and protection every day of our lives. A little flock is full of dependent creatures. A little flock is prone to wander. A little flock is not especially intelligent, and is easily given to panic.

And you know what a sheep does to defend itself, right? Nothing. The little flock has no defense mechanism. The helplessness and dependence of sheep help us to understand the character and the work of the Good Shepherd. One of the marks of a skillful shepherd is the ability to treat every affliction the sheep encounter. With such a good shepherd as Christ guiding us all our days, none of his sheep should be afraid.

Our Father. The Father of Jesus is our Father too. The Father welcomes us to his family and loves us with the same love he has for his eternal Son. He is a good Father, full of affection and care. Jesus emphasizes the Fatherhood of God as the solution to our fears and anxieties.

Our King. He is sovereign and in control. If God were only Shepherd and Father, he might be inclined to do us good but not have the power to do so. If he were only King, he might be powerful but not inclined to do us good. God is sovereign *and* gracious. He is the kind of king who gives his kingdom to his subjects! Through our union with Christ, we have become heirs with Christ and will receive all the privileges and blessings of his kingdom. The kingdom is yours. Provision is yours. God is yours, and you are his.

This is the word of Christ to our troubled souls today: "Fear not, little flock, for it is your Father's good pleasure to give you the kingdom."

John Flavel writes, "If we thoroughly understand and believe what power is in God's hand to defend us, what tenderness is in his heart to help us, and what faithfulness is in his promises, our hearts will be calm—our courage will grow stronger and our fear will grow weaker."[3]

That is our prayer as Jesus speaks to our fears: May our hearts be calm. May our courage grow stronger. May our fear grow weaker. May we be empowered by the word of Christ and the ministry of the Spirit to face a bright future with confidence in God.

Questions for Reflection

1. What makes Jesus so well qualified to speak to our fears?

2. Why is it important to distinguish between faith and natural optimism?

Chapter 3
More Grace Will Come

*God provides for our future needs
by giving us future grace*

ONE MORNING WHEN my daughter Aggie was weak from battling cancer and our family was more exhausted than we have ever been, my wife read a Charles Spurgeon quote to me from the book *Beside Still Waters*. (Of all the commendable things you can look for in a spouse, add this to your list: find someone who asks if she can read Spurgeon quotes to you.)

Meghan read to me that morning through tears. They were tears of sorrow, tears of comfort, tears of hope.

> We have great demands, but Christ has great supplies. Between here and heaven, we may have greater wants than we have yet known. But all along the journey, every resting place is ready; provisions are laid up, good cheer is stored, and nothing has been overlooked. The commissary of the Eternal is absolutely perfect.[1]

Military posts usually include a commissary, which is a store for food and supplies. Our needs are many, but Christ knows our needs and has already prepared to meet them. He goes before us and promises to supply us with grace along the way.

Do you believe that? Resting places are waiting for *you*. Provisions are laid up for *you*. Fresh supplies of peace, joy, and hope are waiting for *you*. In the Lord's kindness, nothing has been overlooked. Future grace is waiting.

John Piper, who wrote an entire book on the idea of future grace, says, "My hope for future goodness and future glory is future grace."[2]

The Manna Principle

In Exodus 16, God's people were in the wilderness and in need of provisions. They had left Egypt nearly two months earlier, and now they feared that they would starve in the wilderness.

God promised that he would send bread, called manna, from heaven. But he commanded them to only gather a day's portion every day. When the bread came, Moses told them to make sure that none was left over for the next day. They were to take only what could be eaten that same morning.

As we so often do, God's people failed to listen. When the sun grew hot, the extra manna bred worms and stank. Soon they learned: for the next forty years, until they came to the land of Canaan, the people gathered their manna morning by morning.

This is the manna principle: *God gives grace for today, and tomorrow will bring new mercies.* We are God's wilderness people, journeying to the Promised Land of heaven. Like Israel, we often doubt that we will make it. Like Israel, we are often quick to distrust the providence, goodness, and wisdom of God. Like Israel, we often forget that God is the God of tomorrow, and the God of future grace.

In *The Pilgrim's Progress*, the man named Christian was made to walk the hill called Difficulty. But at the bottom of the hill was a spring, where Christian was able to drink and find refreshment. He spoke to himself as he started up the hill, calling himself to neither faint nor fear. But the hill became much steeper. Christian slowed from running to walking, then fell from walking to crawling on his hands and knees, because the hill was so steep.

But then: "About half way up the hill there was a pleasant arbor built by the Lord of the hill for the refreshment of weary travelers."[3]

A pleasant arbor, purposefully placed for the weary soul in need of refreshment. The lesson? If God calls you to travel the hill of difficulty, he will graciously provide pleasant arbors for you along the way.

I am currently on my own hill of difficulty, but God has been true to his Word and has not left me without times of refreshing and peace. Isaiah 49:10 says, "They shall not hunger or thirst, neither scorching wind nor sun shall strike them, for he who has pity on them will lead them, and by springs of water will guide them."

God gives sufficient grace for today, and each new day is met with fresh grace in Christ from the loving hand of our Father.

Sometimes you might lie in bed at night and think, *I'm not going to make it though the week.* Or we look at the circumstances of others and think, *If I suffered that way, I would never survive. If I experienced that loss, I couldn't go on.*

The problem is, we are making calculations without fresh supplies of grace in view.

Fear of the future is always the result of forgetting future grace. J. C. Ryle says, "If tomorrow brings a cross, He who sends it can and will send grace to bear it."[4] We have not been given the grace for every possible circumstance; we have been given grace and will be given grace for the circumstances we actually face. God provides for our future needs by giving us future grace.

Do you believe that God will give you the grace you need for everything he calls you to and everything he brings your way? It is not a question concerning your faithfulness, but God's faithfulness to his promises concerning you. Do you believe that his mercies are new every morning (Lamentations 3:22–23), that his goodness and mercy will follow you all the days of your life (Psalm 23:6), that he waits to be gracious to you (Isaiah 30:18)?

In Christ, we learn that unexpected trials and changes will be accompanied by new strength. Trusting in future grace means knowing that God says to us what he said to Moses: "My presence will go with you, and I will give you rest" (Exodus 33:14).

A World of Change

One reason we must have firm convictions regarding future grace is because change is sure to come. The passing of time always brings change, from childhood to old age.

The Pixar movie *Inside Out* is not only a study in emotions, it is also a reflection on change in the life of a young person. An eleven-year-old girl named Riley is uprooted from her Midwestern life in Minnesota, where she enjoys a good life of friendship, hockey, and a great home and yard. Her family relocates to San Francisco when her dad gets a new job. Her new life is soon disappointing, and she has difficulty coping with the massive changes of new school, new people, new home, new life.

Riley begins to feel the loss of the stability she had always known. All of her emotions (who are main characters in the story, named Anger, Sadness, Disgust, Fear, and Joy) start to disagree with one another on how to handle the changes of life. Little by little, things begin to fall apart as Riley fails to cope with change. She distances herself from her parents and her friends, and inside of her there are "personality islands" that begin to crumble and fall. Her life is not what it once was, and she is not the person she once was.

The Pixar movie *Up* also addresses the theme of change. In this film, the focus is not on the life of a young girl, but on the life of an old man. Carl Fredricksen is an elderly widower. He met his wife, Ellie, when they were young, and she told him about her desire to have a house on a cliff overlooking Paradise Falls.

A four-minute, stunningly beautiful montage without dialogue tells the story of their wedding, their miscarriage and inability to have children, the financial challenges that prevented them from going to Paradise Falls, the reality of growing old together, and the sorrow of saying goodbye to the one with whom you have shared your life and dreams.

When he is seventy-eight years old, Carl ties thousands of balloons to his house to travel to South America and keep the promise he made to Ellie, who has passed away: their house will be planted by Paradise Falls.

Change comes to us as well. There are no promises that my family, my job, my health, or my house will remain unchanged. In fact, my kids will grow up, my job will someday be performed by someone else, my health will slowly fail me, and my house will not be my home forever.

Yet none of this needs to be depressing, because the most important things in life will never change. And for every change, the character and grace of Christ remain constant.

The best way to prepare for life's changes is to remember that God's grace is unchanging. The reason we can be confident that grace is unchanging is because Christ is unchanging, and he is the fountain of all grace.

Hebrews 13:8 celebrates the immutability of the Lord Jesus Christ. The author has just urged us to avoid the love of money (v. 5); he has spoken to the reality of fear (v. 6); he has reminded us of our leaders who have gone ahead of us to glory and are no longer with us (v. 7). Then, there is this majestic statement regarding the one who never changes: "Jesus Christ is the same yesterday, today, and forever."

"Forever" has the entirety of our future in view. If God is not subject to change through time or circumstances, then his gracious character and gracious treatment of us will always remain the same.

It is a mistake to think that grace is only a thing of the past. Whatever comes your way, grace will find you. Whatever you experience, grace will be with you.

Greater than We Know

Without minimizing the glory of Christ's finished work, we need to recapture a sense of the glory of his present and future work. Never stop talking about when you were saved by grace, but then go on to talk about how you are presently being saved by grace and will one day be fully saved by grace.

Grace is greater than we know, and we should learn to mine the riches of God's future grace. The benefits of grace that you have experienced thus far are glorious, but are surpassed by the benefits yet to come.

Past grace builds confidence in future grace. We should not minimize the role of gratitude for past grace as a biblical motivation for living the Christian life. The grace we have already experienced should promote a life of humility and praise (1 Timothy 1:12–17), the love Christ has already shown ought to control us (2 Corinthians 5:14), and we must present ourselves to God as living sacrifices in response to God's great mercies (Romans 12:1).

At the same time, we must never treat grace as a thing of the past. Grace is amazing, as John Newton observes, not only because it has brought us safe thus far, but also because it will lead us home.

There is a stunning example of the scope of grace in Acts 20. The apostle Paul is preparing the church in Ephesus for his absence. He had previously ministered in Ephesus for several years, and he now gathers the elders of the Ephesian church in Miletus. He speaks with an awareness of the great duties and dangers they will face. He knows that he is likely to never see them again in this life.

Paul doesn't make the mistake of thinking that their growth depends on him. Nor does he allow the dangers and duties they face to loom larger than the power of grace. Rather, he views them and their future in light of the superior power of future grace.

He says in Acts 20:32, "And now I commend you to God and to the word of his grace, which is able to build you up and to give you the inheritance among all those who are sanctified."

To commend means to entrust, to commit to another, to hand over for safekeeping. Paul says that he commends or entrusts these Christians to the grace of God. We are entrusted to grace! What more do we need? Without this grace, the smallest duty would be too great for us, and the slightest trial would overwhelm us. But when we have even the smallest amount of grace, we are empowered to do and bear all things.

Through Acts 20:32 God speaks to us, reminding us that his grace is powerful to build us up, to sustain us, and to keep us to the end. The word of grace has not saved us only to then leave us to ourselves. Grace continues its work in us! The conquest of grace has not only *brought* you to Christ (in the past), it *is building* you up (in the present) and *will one day bring* you safely home.

We believe in the immeasurable riches of God's grace to us in Christ. We believe in a grace that justifies—yes, but not only that! We believe in a grace that sanctifies. We believe in a grace that empowers us for godly living, a grace that breaks the power of canceled sin. And we believe in a grace that glorifies! We believe in a grace that will give us the inheritance among all those who are sanctified, and we have set our hope fully on the grace that will be brought to us at the revelation of Jesus Christ (1 Peter 1:13).

Grace for Every Need

One implication of the reality of future grace is that we should learn to praise God for the grace he has yet to give. Charles Spurgeon observes,

> This is how to deal with God. Praise Him before you are delivered. Praise Him for what is coming. Adore Him for what He is going to do. I do not think there is

a sweeter song in God's ear than the song of one who blesses Him for grace that has not yet been tasted, who blesses Him for answers that have not been received but are sure to come. The praise for past gratitude is sweet, but even sweeter is the praise of full confidence that all will be well.[5]

We must also remember that in Christ, we will always have access to future grace for whatever needs may come. It is not right that children would be reluctant to ask a father for help, or that weak sinners would hesitate to go to the throne of grace.

There is now and always will be *forgiving grace* when sin gets the upper hand. Ephesians 1:7 celebrates the forgiveness of all our trespasses according to the riches of God's grace.

There will be *empowering grace* to walk in faith and obedience. "You then, my child, be strengthened by the grace that is in Christ Jesus" (2 Timothy 2:1).

There will be *comforting grace* in the midst of every sorrow and loss. Grace and peace come to us in Christ from "the Father of mercies and God of all comfort" (2 Corinthians 1:2–3).

There will be *delivering grace* to rescue us from danger. In 2 Timothy 4:18, Paul says "The Lord will rescue me from every evil deed and bring me safely into his heavenly kingdom."

There will be *sustaining grace* as you face trials of many kinds. There are times when we are not spared hardship, weaknesses, and calamity. Instead the Lord promises us, "My grace is sufficient for you, for my power is made perfect in weakness" (2 Corinthians 12:9). Sometimes sustaining grace, which upholds us through a trial, is a greater testimony to the power of God than delivering grace, which removes the trial from us.

There will be *guiding grace* as you make decisions about the future. The Lord promises, "I will instruct you and teach you in the way you should go; I will counsel you with my eye upon you" (Psalm 32:8).

There will be *renewing grace* that ushers you into eternal glory. "And after you have suffered a little while, the God of all grace, who has called you to his eternal glory in Christ, will himself restore, confirm, strengthen, and establish you" (1 Peter 5:10).

There will be *rewarding grace* when you stand before the judgment seat of Christ. "Then each one will receive his commendation from God" (1 Corinthians 4:5). God will reward you by grace for the good he has produced in you by grace. Your works will be imperfect, and you will not be deserving of reward, but God will graciously give it.

What else do we need, if we have God's future grace throughout our lives? We are poor in ourselves, but we will find riches of grace in Christ. We are tired in ourselves, but we will be energized by his grace. We are weak in ourselves, but we will be supernaturally strengthened by the grace that is in Christ Jesus.

Benedictions: Grace Goes with You

I love the great benedictions of Scripture. Benedictions are often spoken in churches, extending hope, encouragement, and grace to God's people as they leave the service. It is good to ensure that we leave our gatherings as Christians primarily aware of what God has done for us and all he will continue to do for us in Christ.

Every benediction speaks a divine blessing over the people of God in the form of a prayer. These words are a reminder that the God of all grace is with us, waiting to be gracious to us and eager to act on our behalf. I commend to you a study of the benedictions of Scripture.

- Numbers 6:24–26 is the great benediction of the Old Testament, reminding God's people of his future grace: "The LORD bless you and keep you; the LORD make his face to shine upon you and be gracious to you; the LORD lift up his countenance upon you and give you peace."

- The Trinitarian benediction at the end of 2 Corinthians is simple, elegant, and glorious: "The grace of the Lord Jesus Christ and the love of God and the fellowship of the Holy Spirit be with you all" (2 Corinthians 13:14).
- First Thessalonians 5:23–24 reminds us that God's grace is faithfully working a complete sanctification that will be realized when Christ returns. "Now may the God of peace himself sanctify you completely, and may your whole spirit and soul and body be kept blameless at the coming of our Lord Jesus Christ. He who calls you is faithful; he will surely do it."

Here is one more benediction from Hebrews 13:20–21. It's a glorious reminder that the grace of God will equip you to do his will, that his grace is powerfully at work in you, and that resurrection hope and the eternal covenant are yours by his grace.

Now may the God of peace who brought again from the dead our Lord Jesus, the great shepherd of the sheep, by the blood of the eternal covenant, equip you with everything good that you may do his will, working in us that which is pleasing in his sight, through Jesus Christ, to whom be glory forever and ever. Amen.

Questions for Reflection

1. How does the truth that Christ is unchanging help us in the midst of changing circumstances?

2. Charles Spurgeon exhorts Christians to praise God for grace that has yet to come. Take time to thank God for some of the ways you will experience his grace in the future.

Chapter 4

The Power of Hope

*Hope is the confident expectation
of what is guaranteed to happen*

OUTSIDE MY OFFICE hangs a print of a famous painting created by George Frederic Watts in 1886. It's entitled *Hope*. A woman sits alone on a globe and her head is bowed in sorrow. Her eyes are bandaged; she cannot see the way forward. She holds a harp-like instrument called a lyre. Every string is broken except for one.

The broken strings represent the disappointments and injustices of life: our shattered expectations, our despair, our failures, our brokenness. The one remaining string is the string of hope: the hope that beautiful music will again fill this world and fill our lives. The hope of a better future.

Martin Luther King Jr. talked about the painting in a 1959 sermon called "Shattered Dreams." After describing the painting, King asked, "Is there any one of us who has not faced the agony of blasted hopes and shattered dreams?" If we haven't yet, we will soon enough.

King observed that we don't naturally respond to suffering and disappointment with hope. We turn instead to the enemies of hope:

- Bitterness: a complaining, fault-finding posture toward God, life, and other people.

- Withdrawal: a tendency to turn inward and become detached from reality.
- Fatalism: a "whatever" attitude that concludes that our choices and circumstances are meaningless.

In the remainder of that message, King went on to preach the message of hope. "What, then, is the answer? The answer lies in our willing acceptance of unwanted and unfortunate circumstances even as we still cling to a radiant hope, our acceptance of finite disappointment even as we adhere to infinite hope."[1]

An Anchor, a Helmet, and a Door

Theologian Herman Bavinck states, "The life of believers is totally sustained and guided by hope."[2] If we are to be sustained and guided as God intends, we must study what his Word reveals about this hope.

The Bible uses the imagery of an anchor, a helmet, and a door to describe our hope.

An anchor. Hebrews 6:19–20 says that hope is "a sure and steadfast anchor of the soul, a hope that enters into the inner place behind the curtain, where Jesus has gone as a forerunner on our behalf." The anchor of hope gives security in the storms of life. God's eternal purpose for us is as sure as Christ's eternal priesthood.

Christian hope is not to be confused with wishful thinking. Hope is not an uncertain expectation of something that may or may not happen. Rather, hope is a realistic expectation and joyful anticipation of the good that is guaranteed to come for all who are in Christ. Hope is a reminder that the best is yet to come. Jeremiah Burroughs says, "We have great things in hand, but greater things in hope."[3]

A helmet. In the context of describing the coming day of the Lord, 1 Thessalonians 5:8–9 says that we have put on "for a helmet the hope of salvation. For God has not destined us for wrath, but to obtain salvation through our Lord Jesus Christ." Our Savior died for us to secure our hope in him. And this sure hope of our final salvation in the age to come is a helmet that we have put on here and now.

This is a comfort to us when our hope is dim. However battered we may be in the war, however much despair has the upper hand, however bleak the future seems, by God's grace we have this helmet of the hope of salvation. In Christ, you have put it on. Your helmet has already sustained many blows and it has not failed you.

What does a helmet do? It protects us in battle against our enemies, which are the world, the flesh, and the Devil. This helmet preserves our lives and guards our thinking. A helmet doesn't mean that you will never go to battle, but it does mean that you will be protected *in* battle. Knowing that we are protected by hope emboldens us. We go bravely into war, fighting a good fight, led by Christ our Captain, because we have been armed with the helmet of hope.

A door. Hosea 2:15 says that God makes the Valley of Achor a door of hope. That means he loves to take the places of trouble in our lives and transform them into places of grace.

This changes the way we view present and future trials. The Puritan William Gurnall says that "Hope never produces more joy than in affliction."[4] "Hope," he adds, "is God's messenger that speaks to the person who has concluded he will never be able to outlive such a rough tide of affliction. Hope lifts his head above the surging waves and says, 'Go, for your God will be with you.'"[5]

When trouble surrounds us and surging waves pound against our souls, hope will be there to lift your head. What seems to be an unending valley of hardship leads to a door of hope. In the darkest hour, God does not abandon us; he assures us that he is near.

The Future Controls the Present

Tim Keller once gave an illustration that demonstrates the energizing power of hope. Imagine that there are two women who are identical in age, socioeconomic status, education level, and temperament. They are both hired to be part of a tedious assembly line, doing work that is repetitive and boring. They do this work over and over for eight hours each day. They are placed in identical rooms, with the same lighting, temperature, and ventilation. They have the same number of breaks.

Their circumstances are identical except for one difference: One woman has been told that at the end of the year she will be paid thirty thousand dollars, and the other woman has been told that she will be paid thirty million dollars.

After a few weeks, one woman is going crazy and wants to quit. The other is working full of joy. What makes the difference can be reduced to one factor: their expectation of the future. Keller says, "What we believe about our future completely controls how we are experiencing our present."[6]

This is the energizing power of hope. Hope not only means a better future, it invades the present with joy and faith. It empowers us to face anything. It's why we pray, "May the God of hope fill you with all joy and peace in believing, so that by the power of the Holy Spirit you may abound in hope" (Romans 15:13).

Maybe the Best of Things

When the movie *The Shawshank Redemption* was first released in 1994, no one predicted that within a few years' time it would be voted Best Film of the Nineties and that people would rank the movie in the Top Five Best Films of all time, alongside *Star Wars*, *The Godfather*, *Raiders of the Lost Ark*, and *Jaws*.

Writer and director Frank Darabont says that he regularly receives mail from people who say that the movie helped them survive a difficult relationship, or got them through a really bad illness, or helped them hang on when a loved one died.

It's been over twenty years since its release, and it still tops all the lists of inspirational movies. The movie is about the sustaining power of hope in the midst of suffering. It's the story of a banker named Andy, who is convicted of a murder he did not commit. He maintains his innocence and survives nineteen years in Shawshank State Prison in Maine. The prison is full of despair, but Andy has an unshakable, hope-filled outlook that gives him peace and joy, and enables him to survive mistreatment, suffering, and the injustice of his imprisonment. At one point he tells a friend, "Hope is a good thing, maybe the best of things, and no good thing ever dies."

Scripture speaks of this good and living hope. The resurrection of Christ has ignited a hope in those who belong to him. God desires this hope to rage with glory and power in the heart of every believer. It is not only a *good hope* (2 Thessalonians 2:16); it is a *living hope* (1 Peter 1:3).

First Peter was written to those who, like us, are "grieved by various trials" (1 Peter 1:6). In the midst of trials, God reminds us of our living hope for the future, and grounds this hope firmly in the resurrection of Jesus Christ. Our hope is alive because Christ is alive. Jesus Christ has risen from the dead, and so long as he lives, our hope can never die.

> Blessed be the God and Father of our Lord Jesus Christ! According to his great mercy, he has caused us to be born again to a living hope through the resurrection of Jesus Christ from the dead, to an inheritance that is imperishable, undefiled, and unfading, kept in heaven for you, who by God's power are being guarded through faith for a salvation ready to be revealed in the last time. (1 Peter 1:3–5)

Scripture has a lot to say about this hope.

- Our hope is a *bold hope*. Second Corinthians 3:12 says, "Since we have such a hope, we are very bold."
- Our hope is an *unashamed hope*. Romans 5 says we can rejoice in our sufferings, because hardships are ultimately producing a hope that will never "put us to shame" (v. 5).
- Our hope is a *blessed hope*. Titus 2:13 says that we are "waiting for our blessed hope, the appearing of the glory of our great God and Savior Jesus Christ." This is our joy: We know without a doubt that the one who gave himself for us will return for us!
- Our hope is a *saving hope*. Romans 8:23–24 says, "And not only the creation, but we ourselves, who have the firstfruits of the Spirit, groan inwardly as we wait eagerly for adoption as sons, the redemption of our bodies. For in this hope we were saved."
- Our hope is a *purifying hope*. The hope that we will one day be conformed to the image of Christ makes us more like him now. "Beloved, we are God's children now, and what we will be has not yet appeared; but we know that when he appears we shall be like him, because we shall see him as he is. And everyone who thus hopes in him purifies himself as he is pure" (1 John 3:2–3).
- Our hope is a *heavenly hope*. God assures us that this hope is out of the reach of every threat. It cannot be lost; it is "the hope laid up for you in heaven" (Colossians 1:5).

Remember that we were once without hope. We were separated from Christ and therefore numbered among those "having no hope and without God in the world" (Ephesians 2:12). What changed? You did not find hope; hope found you! "But now in Christ . . ." (Ephesians 2:13). Now in Christ, we are the people of hope!

Christ shed his blood for our justification, giving us full confidence that we will be saved by him from the wrath of God. Christ rose from the dead, assuring that we too will rise in union with him. Christ ascended to the Father, where he sovereignly reigns over every page of history to ensure that all things are placed in subjection to him. Christ sent the Holy Spirit as a guarantee of our future inheritance.

Hope Lives On

True Christianity is a life of hopeful expectation, resolute confidence, and absolute joy regarding the future. It is the mark of a Christian to "rejoice in hope" (Romans 12:12). Yet the grounds for our rejoicing are not the absence of trials, but the presence of hope in Christ and his finished work. "The hope of the righteous brings joy" (Proverbs 10:28).

This is one of the beautiful things about Christianity. The Bible is utterly realistic about the brokenness and pain of this world and, at the same time, it is full of hope regarding the future because of Christ. God says to his people today what he said to Israel through the prophet Jeremiah: "There is hope for your future" (Jeremiah 31:17). And this hope is what sustains us through grief and trials of many kinds.

One reason the music of Andrew Peterson ministers so deeply to me is his treatment of the theme of hope. He has an album called *The Burning Edge of Dawn*, which has been the soundtrack of my life these days. In a song called "The Dark Before the Dawn," Peterson describes the forward-looking nature of hope. One day the sun will rise, and shadows will scatter and dragons will flee.

But for now? Our present experience, Peterson sings, is often pain and tears and darkness. And so we wait. Because when all we see is darkness, still we know the dawn is coming.

Not every song the Christian sings ends with exuberance and shouts of joy. Sometimes all we can sing is that our hope has not died. We are still standing. And our standing is a testimony to the power of hope.

It's not so much that we are holding on to hope as it is that the God of hope is holding on to us. I might fail to remember, apply, and live in the good of my hope as I should, but the God of hope will not fail to remember me. Praise his name, he will forever hold me fast.

Embracing Lament

Looking to the future with hope-filled confidence in Christ doesn't remove sorrow and lament from our lives. A future of hardship is a heavy burden, and hope does not turn every thought about the future into a happy thought, or transform every emotion about the future into a happy feeling. Life in a fallen world is full of lament.

And yet, lament is not opposed to hope; it is an expression of hope. Todd Billings explains, "As strange as it sounds, the fact that the psalmist can bring anger, frustration, and protest to God is rooted in hope: if you don't hope that God is good and sovereign, you don't bother to bring your lament and thanksgiving to the Lord."[7] Kelly Kapic says that hope without lament is naïve optimism and lament without hope is unrelenting despair. It is hope and lament together that marks faithful living and suffering.[8]

Jesus invites us to follow in his footsteps of lament. He is the Man of Sorrows, weeping at the news of Lazarus's death, mourning over Jerusalem, grieving in the garden, crying out from the cross.

The book of Lamentations is full of grief, darkness, and feelings of hopelessness. "My soul is bereft of peace; I have forgotten what happiness is; so I say, 'My endurance has perished; so has my hope from the LORD'" (Lamentations 3:17–18). At times, sorrow surrounds us and our afflictions are all we can see.

41

Hopelessness is an invitation to place our hope in the One who will never fail us or disappoint us. It is in the midst of lament that hope emerges. Lamentations 3:21–24 says,

> But this I call to mind,
>> and therefore I have hope:
> The steadfast love of the LORD never ceases;
>> his mercies never come to an end;
> they are new every morning;
>> great is your faithfulness.
> "The LORD is my portion," says my soul,
>> "therefore I will hope in him."

Grow in Hope

What if we find that our hope is still weak? How can we grow in hope? Here are a few suggestions:

Feed your hope on the written Word. Romans 15:4 says that "whatever was written in former days was written for our instruction, that through endurance and through the encouragement of the Scriptures we might have hope." Those who abound in hope are those who consistently abide in the Word.

Look often to Calvary. Hope is strengthened by seeing the love of God displayed in the cross of Christ. Strong hope comes from fierce convictions regarding the good character of God, and that goodness is proven once-for-all in the giving of his beloved Son. "He who did not spare his own Son but gave him up for us all, how will he not also with him graciously give us all things?" (Romans 8:32).

Share your struggles for hope with a trusted friend. Sharing our challenges with others is never easy, but it's worth it because we know that God "gives grace to the humble" (James 4:6).

Surround yourself with hope-filled people. The church is one body, and the people of Christ share one hope (Ephesians 4:4). We can't grow in hope if we remain in isolation.

Study the object of your hope. John Owen says that the reason Christians don't benefit more from the grace that comes through hope "is because they do not abide in thoughts and contemplation of the things hoped for."[9] Consider reading books that set your mind on the good news of your future in Christ. Read *We Shall See God: Charles Spurgeon's Classic Devotional Thoughts on Heaven*, by Randy Alcorn. Or read Alcorn's book *Heaven*, or his shorter book *In Light of Eternity*. Read *The Saints' Everlasting Rest*, by Richard Baxter, and *Christ and the Future* by Cornelis Venema.

Consider the promises of God. Are you familiar with the "precious and very great promises" of God (2 Peter 1:4)? Have you considered how the promises of God are to be used in the Christian life? We devote the next chapter to this great theme.

Questions for Reflection

1. How does hope for the future change us in the present?

2. What is the relationship between lament and hope?

Chapter 5

Using the Promises

God is the great Promise-Keeper
whose words will never fail

I WANT TO be like the mighty saints of Hebrews 11, those men and women who triumphantly overcame as they learned to live by faith in the promises of God. I want to live every day as one seeking a better country, a promised homeland. I want to live with my heart less controlled by fear and more captivated by future rewards. I want to face tomorrow and every day of my life with confidence in the faithful character of God, undaunted by the mouths of lions, the power of fire, the edge of the sword, torture, imprisonment, enemies, and affliction. (See Hebrews 11:32–38.) I want to be made strong out of weakness and mighty in war. I want to be numbered among those of whom the world is not worthy.

In other words, I want to be like Joni Eareckson Tada.

Made Defiant by the Promises

Joni is a hero of mine because she has faced an extraordinarily difficult life with radiant joy in Christ. The promises of God are her sword and shield, and she has learned to wield the promises every day.

Growing up, Joni was very active. She loved riding horses, hiking, tennis, and swimming. But she had a diving accident as a teenager and became a quadriplegic, paralyzed from the shoulders down. That was on July 30, 1967, just over fifty years ago.

Anger, fear, and depression assailed her. Through it all and to this day, Christ has sustained her. God has taught her how to fight for faith by using the promises of God. By relying on the promises, she has faced a difficult future with defiant joy and staggering courage.

Joni says that she can often hear her pain nagging at her and taunting her: "Yeah, yeah, you say that God is good, but come on, look at you, you're paralyzed with quadriplegia; you're in a wheelchair, you can hardly do anything for yourself, and on top of all that, you feel that knife into your hip and lower back. That's me, your old friend pain, just reminding you that you've got nothing to be happy about. Nothing! If you stand back and look at yourself, you've got to admit it, Joni, you're a miserable, sorry sight. So go on, curse God and die."

She says, "That's what pain tries to tell me. But you know what? I have learned not to listen. What's more, I've learned to fight back with joy. I take joy, the Holy Spirit's gift to me, and I hold it up in from of my pain and say, 'Look, I may be wasting away on the outside, but inside I am being renewed. I'm being renewed by the promise of my salvation; by the promise of God's grace; by the promise that my godly response to you, pain, will win me a rich reward in heaven. I have the joy of the Lord and he is my strength. I have joy that is real and rock solid, unshakable and unmovable, all because of Jesus and his promises. So you take that, pain.'"[1]

This joyful courage and faith-filled outlook on the future is not beyond you, because Joni's God is your God, and the promises she clings to are promises God has made to you as well.

The promises of God make us defiant; we resist temptation, fight depression, and destroy condemnation, all by the power of the promises.

Have you learned to take the promises God has made and put them to use in your life?

Charles Spurgeon says, "The promises of God are to the believer an inexhaustible mine of wealth. Happy is it for him if he knows how to search out their secret veins and enrich himself with their hidden treasures. They are to him an armory containing all manner of offensive and defensive weapons."[2]

What should we do when we are tempted to doubt the good character of God and to distrust the good purposes of God for our future? Go to the armory and pick up the promises of God.

These promises in Scripture do not trickle down slowly and sparsely upon us. They come at us like water from a fire hose, blasting us with blessing, refreshment, and hope. Faith in the promises is calculated to fill our souls with security and joy.

Some promises pertain to all people, and some apply only to Christians. Some promises are temporal and therefore fulfilled in this present age, and some are eternal and fulfilled only in the age to come. Some promises are conditional upon our obedience and some are unconditional. But all of the promises are of great value in facing the future.

"You've Taken a Great Deal Off My Mind"

There is a *Peanuts* (Charlie Brown) comic strip that perfectly captures the functional value of God's promises. Lucy and Linus are having a conversation. Lucy sits looking out the window, and it is pouring outside. She says to Linus, "Boy, look at it rain . . . what if it floods the whole world?"

Linus very calmly and matter-of-factly says, "It will never do that. In the ninth chapter of Genesis, God promised Noah that it would never happen again, and the sign of the promise is the rainbow."

Lucy, quite relieved by this, says, "You've taken a great deal off my mind."

Linus replies, "Sound theology has a way of doing that!"[3]

Every promise God has made should take a great deal of worry off our minds. Sound theology, including all that God has promised, is intended to make a difference in our lives. So many of the problems we face can be traced back to our failure to live as though the promises of God are true. If we lose sight of God's promises, we will inevitably lose our sense of courage.

John Calvin understood that the Christian life is lived by faith in the promises of God. He says, "We ought to be armed with God's promises, so that we may with courageous hearts follow wherever he may call us."[4]

In his commentary on the book of Joshua, Calvin draws what has been for me a life-changing principle from Joshua 10:8. In Joshua 10, many kings had gathered their great armies against a place called Gibeon. The men of Gibeon called for Joshua, and Joshua came to help. That is when the Lord drew near to Joshua and said that he would fight for them and secure the victory of his people: "And the Lord said to Joshua, 'Do not fear them, for I have given them into your hands. Not a man of them shall stand before you'" (Joshua 10:8). The next verse says that Joshua took action and came suddenly upon his enemies.

Here is Calvin's simple but extraordinary insight on this verse. He says, "God stimulates us more powerfully to the performance of duty by promising than by ordering."[5]

That is a remarkable statement. Commandments tell us our duty. Ordering or commanding is an essential part of guiding Christians in the performance of our duties. Promises, on the other hand, reveal not what we must do, and not what God will attempt to do, but what God has bound himself to do for us. He has told us what he will most certainly do prior to having done it, for the sake of strengthening our faith and calling us to action.

How does God motivate us most powerfully to obedience? Not by ordering, and certainly not by threatening, but by promising. Too many Christians try to live off commandments and threats alone, thereby robbing themselves of greater comfort, courage, and conformity to the image of Christ. In the promises we find the power to do all that God calls us to do.

Not One Word Has Failed

The entire book of Joshua is a valuable study on the promises of God. Joshua was written to persuade us of the power of our promise-keeping God. The main lesson of the book of Joshua is not human courage or morality, but divine faithfulness. The Lord is a warrior who fights for us and will not fail to keep his word to us. The King of glory is mighty in battle. That is the point of the book of Joshua.

After the death of Moses, Joshua faced the overwhelming task of leading the people of God into the Promised Land. The way was hard, the people were sinful, and the land was occupied by great enemies. The Lord reminded Joshua of his promises. The promise of land was first given to Abraham, Isaac, and Jacob, then to Moses, and now to Joshua.

God also promised that he would be with Joshua, and there is no greater promise than the promise of his presence. "Just as I was with Moses, so I will be with you. I will not leave you or forsake you" (1:5). In Hebrews 13:5–6, the promise of Joshua 1:5 is applied directly to new covenant Christians. God is with us today! His presence is the source of the strength and courage he commands. Fear and dismay are driven out by the promise that God is with us (Joshua 1:9).

In chapter 2, spies are sent to examine the land of promise. That experience confirms the word of God to his people, and they say to Joshua, "Truly the Lord has given all the land into our hands" (2:24). God takes action to bolster our faith in the future he has promised us.

When Israel crosses the Jordan, they create a memorial to remind future generations that God is faithful to his promises (chapter 4). The generation that wandered in the wilderness was disobedient (5:6), yet their sin is a reminder to us that even our unbelief cannot deter the fulfillment of God's promises for us.

Before Jericho ever falls, God says, "I have given Jericho into your hand" (6:2). The walls still stood. The people of God were weak. Victory seemed impossible. Yet so certain is the victory of God that he assures us of it before we experience it.

God is declaring to his people, "Nothing can deter my promises! Not death, not enemies, not even your sin. Not rivers or walls or great armies or anything else. The word of my power conquers all!"

Hebrews 11:30 celebrates the faith that Joshua and his army had in the promise. God said Jericho would fall, and they believed that his word would not fail. Every wall that fell declared the faithfulness of our promise-keeping God.

In Joshua 15, what at first appears to us to be a boring description of the land is in fact a description of the gift God had promised as an inheritance. This land ultimately points to the heavenly inheritance that will be given to all nations in Christ.

The book of Joshua leaves us praising God for his faithfulness to his promises.

> Thus the LORD gave to Israel all the land that he swore to give to their fathers. And they took possession of it, and they settled there. And the LORD gave them rest on every side just as he had sworn to their fathers. Not one of all their enemies had withstood them, for the LORD had given all their enemies into their hands. Not one word of all the good promises that the LORD had made to the house of Israel had failed; all came to pass. (Joshua 21:43–45)

This same God has promised us land, rest, victory, and the fulfillment of every word he has spoken in Christ. God is the great Promise-Keeper, whose promises reveal his heart and guide us home.

The promises of God will never fail because they are grounded in the unfailing character of God. "God is not man, that he should lie, or a son of man, that he should change his mind. Has he said, and will he not do it? Or has he spoken, and will he not fulfill it?" (Numbers 23:19).

And so the day is coming when we look back on every day of our lives, and every trial we have known on life's weary path, and declare the faithfulness of God to keep every one of his promises to us. Joshua in old age declared it: "And now I am about to go the way of all the earth, and you know in your hearts and souls, all of you, that not one word has failed of all the good things that the LORD your God promised concerning you. All have come to pass for you; not one of them has failed" (Joshua 23:14).

You will declare it too. The promises will never fail.

Precious and Very Great Promises

In 2 Peter 1:4, God tells us that his promises are "precious and very great." The promises of God are *precious* because they have been secured by the precious blood of Christ. As 2 Corinthians 1:20 says, all the promises of God find their Yes in Christ.

These are not only precious promises, they are very great promises. The greatness of God's promises is revealed not only in how they glorify God's character, but also in what he accomplishes through them in our lives. According to 2 Peter 1:3–4, the promises of God are among those things that "pertain to life and godliness." God "has granted to us his great and precious promises, so that through them you may become partakers of the divine nature, having escaped from the corruption that is in the world because of sinful desire."

What effect do the promises have in our lives?

The promises deepen our sense of security in the Father's love. When our feelings tell us that we are forgotten and forsaken, the promises of God in Christ reveal his heart for us. God gave his only

Son for us and he will never forget us. "Can a woman forget her nursing child, that she should have no compassion on the son of her womb? Even these may forget, yet I will not forget you. Behold, I have engraved you on the palms of my hands" (Isaiah 49:15–16).

It is to the fearful, the weak, the mourning, and the oppressed that God pledges his love: "The LORD your God is in your midst, a mighty one who will save; he will rejoice over you with gladness; he will quiet you by his love; he will exult over you with loud singing" (Zephaniah 3:17).

The Puritan William Gurnall says, "The promise is God's love-letter to His bride in which he opens His very heart and tells everything He will do for her."[6]

The promises help us embrace our identity as pilgrims in this world. Hebrews 11:13 says, "These all died in faith, not having received the things promised, but having seen them and greeted them from afar, and having acknowledged that they were strangers and exiles on the earth." We speak in a way that reveals that this world is not our home. We live as those who desire a better country and will surely arrive there.

The promises relieve our anxieties about the future. The Puritan Samuel Clark wrote,

> A fixed, constant attention to the promises, and a firm belief of them, would prevent solicitude and anxiety about the concerns of this life. It would keep the mind quiet and composed in every change, and support and keep up our sinking spirits under the several troubles of life. . . . Christians deprive themselves of their most solid comforts by their unbelief and forgetfulness of God's promises. For there is no extremity so great, but there are promises suitable to it, and abundantly sufficient for our relief in it.[7]

The promises sustain and comfort us in suffering. The psalm-ist knew this well. "Let your steadfast love comfort me accord-ing to your promise to your servant" (Psalm 119:76). "Uphold me according to your promise" (Psalm 119:116). "My eyes are awake before the watches of the night, that I may meditate on your promise" (Psalm 119:148).

John Flavel writes, "In the written Word, there are all sorts of refreshing, strengthening, and heart-reviving promises. By his care and wisdom, God prepared these for our relief in days of darkness and trouble."[8]

We have the promise that Christ is our Great High Priest, who sympathizes with us and prays for us in the midst of all our sorrows.

The promises help us kill sin and walk in holiness. God promises that the same power that raised Christ from the dead is at work in us, and that his purifying Spirit is at work in us. According to 2 Corinthians 6:16–18, the promises that God will be our God, and we will be his people—that he will welcome us and be a Father to us—motivate us to cleanse ourselves of sin and impurity. Second Corinthians 7:1 says, "Since we have these promises, beloved, let us cleanse ourselves from every defilement of body and spirit, bringing holiness to completion in the fear of God."

The promises give us courage in prayer. When the Lord promised David that his house would be blessed and the Davidic throne would be established forever, David prayed that God would con-firm the word he had spoken. David said,

> "For you, O LORD of hosts, the God of Israel, have made this revelation to your servant, saying 'I will build you a house.' Therefore your servant has found courage to pray this prayer to you. And now, O LORD God, you are God, and your words are true, and you have promised

this good thing to your servant. Now therefore may it please you to bless the house of your servant." (2 Samuel 7:27–29)

Prayer is asking God to bless us on the basis of God's promise to do so. In view of God's promises, we find courage and power in prayer.

"Your Promise Is Well Tried"

In Psalm 119:140, the psalmist celebrates the God who has always kept his promises: "Your promise is well tried, and your servant loves it."

Consider how the promises are kept in Scripture. In Genesis 3:15 God promised to send a Savior to crush the serpent's head, and he did. In Genesis 12:3, God promised to bless the nations through Abraham, and he did. He is the God of the covenants, the great Promise-Keeper! He promised to write his law on our hearts, and he did (Jeremiah 31:33). He promised to place his Spirit within us, and he did. God promised to send a king like David, a suffering servant, Immanuel. And he did! His promise is well-tried, and we praise him for it.

Consider also how the promises of God have been tried and proven in your life. Look over your life and see the faithfulness of God to you in sustaining you, providing for you, and helping you in time of need. Then move forward, looking for opportunities to cling to the promises of God. The way to strengthen our faith is to remember how the promises of God apply to the particulars of our situation. You will not find a condition or face a trial for which there is not a relevant and corresponding promise to comfort and strengthen you.

- Are you called to make great sacrifices on the path of following Christ? Remember his promise in Mark 10:29–30, that anyone who has made sacrifices for his sake and for the gospel will receive back a hundredfold now in this time and in the age to come.

- Does Satan condemn you and call attention to your many sins? "If we confess our sins, he is faithful and just to forgive us our sins and to cleanse us from all unrighteousness" (1 John 1:9).
- Are you concerned that your past sins and mistakes have put you at a disadvantage moving forward? Receive God's promise to restore the years that have been lost (Joel 2:25).
- Does a sense of loneliness and inadequacy surround you? When a good friend of mine lost her husband, she turned often to the promise of Isaiah 41:10. "Fear not, for I am with you; be not dismayed, for I am your God; I will strengthen you, I will help you, I will uphold you with my righteous right hand."
- Are you weary in your work, carrying responsibilities that are a great burden? Remember the promise of Jesus in Matthew 11:28, "Come to me, all who labor and are heavy laden, and I will give you rest."
- Are you anxious about ministry efforts being in vain? Lean on the promise of Isaiah 55:10–11, that God's Word will accomplish all that God intends, and will succeed in producing a great harvest.
- Do you see injustice in the world and are you tempted to revenge? Hold on to the promise of Romans 12:19: "'Vengeance is mine, I will repay,' says the Lord."
- Are you lamenting the apparent triumph of evil? Romans 16:20 promises, "The God of peace will soon crush Satan under your feet."

One day we will stand in the presence of God and, looking back on our lives, we will joyfully declare, "Your promise is well tried, and your servant loves it."

In the meantime, let's take to heart the many promises God has made to us. Let's look more to the promises of God than the problems of life. Let's set our minds on the great and precious promises, and dare to live like every promise will be fulfilled.

The Promise-Keeper has spoken. And to the praise of his great faithfulness, not one word will fail!

Questions for Reflection

1. What difference does God intend his promises to make in our lives?

2. What is one biblical promise that is especially meaningful to you, or that you can apply to a current situation in your life?

Chapter 6

Unfailing Love

Our strong and faithful Savior will keep us to the end

ONE OF BRAZIL'S most famous landmarks dominates the Rio de Janeiro skyline. It's a cross-shaped statue on Mount Corcovado called *Christ the Redeemer*, built between 1922 and 1931. Christ stands tall with arms extended on either side, with nail marks on his hands.

In 1999, a man named Felix Baumgartner scaled the large statue. He looked over the edge of the granite peak and surveyed the distant ground at the bottom of the mountain, nearly 2,500 feet below. Then he walked to the edge of the outstretched arm of Christ and jumped.

He threw himself from the hand of Christ.

Baumgartner is a skydiver, daredevil, and BASE jumper. He is known for the insane, dangerous stunts he performs. For this particular feat, he had to smuggle his parachute on board a small train that takes groups of tourists up the 2,000-foot mountain to visit the statue. A pulley system helped him get on top of the statue, where he jumped from the hand of Jesus.

The Strong Hand of Christ

The story of Felix Baumgartner reminds me of what Jesus says in John 10:28–29: "I give them eternal life, and they will never perish, and no one will snatch them out of my hand. My Father, who has given them to me, is greater than all, and no one is able to snatch them out of the Father's hand."

For many of us, the greatest fears we have involve our perseverance in faith. Some of our deepest insecurities involve the future of our relationship with God. Maybe you feel the inclination to wander from him. Perhaps you have seen friends who once followed Christ now abandon him. Deep down inside we know that, left to ourselves, we would all jump from the loving hand of Christ.

One particular promise of God is so glorious that it demands the focus of an entire chapter. Jesus has promised that he will never let go of his people, and that no power in all the world can sever us from his hand of love.

Many strong forces attempt to snatch us from his hand: darkness and doubt, sickness and suffering, temptations to sin, Satan and all the forces of hell. Each of these, in its own way, seeks to pry open the fingers of our Lord and take us from his hand.

The Bible is honest about the pressures and the difficulties you will face in the future. Paul mentions many of them in Romans 8, an incredible chapter extolling the unbreakable love of God in Christ. The end of the chapter outlines some of the greatest threats to the security and love that we enjoy in the hand of Christ: tribulation, distress, persecution, famine, nakedness, danger, and death.

- *Tribulation* covers trials of many kinds. What if I face some great hardship and don't move toward God but grow bitter and reject him?
- *Distress* can be emotional, psychological, or physical. It includes pain and loneliness.
- *Persecution* is being mistreated by others for allegiance to Christ. What if our culture continues to decline, and Christians are ridiculed, and I don't have the strength to stand for Christ?

- *Famine* and *nakedness* have in view the question of provision: Will I have food and clothing? Will I have enough money to take care of myself and my family?
- And then there is *death*, the last great enemy, which awaits us all.

The Bible does not teach that if God loves you, life will be easy. The power of God's love does not remove all of life's pressures; it equips us to deal with those pressures and sustains us in the midst of them. We do not fix our eyes on the hardships to come, but on the love and power of the hand of Christ.

Jesus says to you today, "I hold you in my hand. I gave my life for you. I showed my love for you in that while you were a sinner, I died for you. And my love for you is not limited to one point in time; it continues on through the entire course of your life and into eternity. I will give you eternal life, you will never perish, and no one will snatch you out of my hand."

Christians should take verses that speak of God's unbreakable love and personalize them. Christ says to me, "I give Jared eternal life, and Jared will never perish, and no one is able to snatch Jared out of my hand." God declares, "Who shall separate Jared from the love of Christ?" and triumphantly answers, "Nothing in all creation!"

Marcus Peter Johnson writes, "Once joined to Christ, believers will never be separated from him. This is not because our grasp on Christ is so strong, but because his grip on us is unbreakable."[1]

Resting in the Obedience of the Son

The Christian's eternal security hinges entirely upon the obedience of the Son of God. In John 6, Jesus says that the whole reason he came into the world is to carry out the Father's will (v. 38). What is the Father's will? "And this is the will of him who sent me, that I should lose nothing of all that he has given me, but raise it up on the last day" (v. 39). His will is that Christ would not lose a single soul of those given to him.

The Father says to the Son, "These are the ones I have chosen. I give them to you. My command is that you lose none of them."

What follows is one of the most beautiful acts of obedience Christ has performed and is now performing from his heavenly throne of love: the obedience of losing none.

Think of it this way: What would it require for someone who has been genuinely regenerated to be lost? It would require that the pre-creation pact made in the Godhead be broken. It would require that the sinless Son of God disobey the Father. It would require that Jesus commit sin and be cast down from his heavenly throne. It would require that Jesus' words be untrue. It would require that his power be weakened, his love be broken, and his death be in vain.

Impossible!

The issue of your ultimate perseverance in the faith is an issue of the obedience of the Son of God. The security of your final salvation rests entirely upon the faithfulness of Jesus Christ. Sam Storms says, "Our security is ultimately dependent on God's character and commitment, not on ours."[2] If you are in Christ, your preservation and future resurrection is as certain as Jesus' obedience. For you to not finish the race would mean not simply that you are a failure, but that Jesus is a failure, and that can never be.

Can Jesus fail the mission he has been given by the Father? Will the Son of God hang his head in eternal shame?

Impossible.

George Matheson was born in Glasgow, Scotland in 1842. By the age of eighteen, he was totally blind. In spite of this disability, he went on to be an accomplished Bible scholar and teacher. He had been engaged to be married as a teenager, but when his fiancée discovered that he was going blind, she left him. He was devastated.

Matheson's sister cared for him in his blindness. But years later, she was engaged to be married and Matheson was reminded of his heartbreak over the relationship he had lost. With his sister entering marriage, the wound was fresh again. He still grieved that his desire to be married had not been fulfilled. Yet he knew that marriage does not complete or satisfy us most deeply. Only the love of Christ can do that.

So the night before his sister's wedding, in the midst of his sorrow and distress, he wrote one of the great hymns of the nineteenth century, "O love that will not let me go, I rest my weary soul in Thee."

There is a love that will never let us go. Weary souls find rest today in knowing that the steadfast love of the Lord endures forever.

God's love is not like human love, which ebbs and flows based on the performance of others. Parents and family members will at times fail in their love for you. Friends too will disappoint and at times break your heart. The love that we know in this world often fails us and comes to an end. But the love of Christ is altogether different. His love is permanent. He has loved me with an everlasting love. He has made me his forever.

Christ loves you far better than you love him. His love does not waver. His love never fails.

God Maintains the Fire

The Bible's teaching about eternal security—the truth that if we are genuinely saved, we cannot lose our salvation—is often misunderstood. We must remember that it is possible for some people to fall away and abandon the faith even when they have exhibited external signs of conversion in the past. The teaching of Scripture is that only those who persevere—continue in their faith—until the end have been truly born again. Hebrews 3:14 says, "For we have come to share in Christ, if indeed we hold our original confidence firm to the end." One of the ways we know we "share in Christ" is whether or not we go on believing, loving, and obeying him.

Eternal security never means "It appeared that I was saved back then, so I must be saved now, even though there is no evidence of it." Rather, eternal security means "I was saved back then and therefore God is ensuring, through the work of the Holy Spirit, that I go on believing Christ, loving Christ, obeying Christ, and relying on him alone for salvation."

Those who are truly born of the Spirit will never ultimately turn their back on God. You might sin grievously, but grace will find you. You might wander from God, but he will bring you back. You might deny the Lord three times like Peter, but you will confess and repent. You might fall and fail again, but you get back up. You might suffer greatly and the darkness threatens to overwhelm you, but no trial will completely extinguish our love for Christ.

Greg Forster explains, "People who are truly converted to God will never fully and finally turn back because God creates in them, by the miraculous power of the Holy Spirit, a love for him that is so powerful it perseveres through all trials. If we are true Christians, our love for God is unbreakable because God's love for us is unbreakable, and his wonder-working power is always at work in us."[3]

Christian, do you believe today that the power of God is at work in you, and that his love for you in unbreakable?

My favorite picture of how God sustains our faith in him is the story of the fireplace in John Bunyan's book, *The Pilgrim's Progress*. The main character, Christian, is about to begin his journey of the Christian life, and he stops by the Interpreter's house. This good man, the Interpreter, takes Christian into a room where there was a fireplace.

"The flames from the fireplace grew larger and hotter even though there was someone continually throwing water on it to try to quench it." Christian said, "What does this mean?" The Interpreter answered:

> "This fire is the work of grace that God accomplishes in the heart; he who throws water on the flames to try to extinguish it is the Devil. But as you see, the fire burns higher and hotter despite his efforts to put it out. Now let me show the reason for that."

The Interpreter took Christian to the other side of the wall, where he saw a Man with a vessel of oil in his hand, from which he secretly funneled oil into the fire. Christian asked, "What does this mean?" The Interpreter answered,

> "This is Christ who continually, with the oil of His grace, maintains the work already begun in the heart. No matter what the Devil tries to do, the gracious work that Christ is doing in the souls of His people only increases. You saw that the Man stood behind the wall to maintain the fire; that is to teach you that it is hard for the one being tempted to see how this work of grace is maintained in the soul."[4]

You may be struggling to see how grace is maintained in you, and you are discouraged. Remember who stands behind that wall, even though we do not see him, and remember what he is doing there. The doctrine of the preservation of the saints, the doctrine of the unbreakable love of God, is that Christ has promised to carry out the Father's will by maintaining the work already begun in your heart.

The orchestration of the Father, the obedience of the Son, and the operation of the Holy Spirit have secured your eternal salvation. This is the unbreakable love of God for you. J. I. Packer says, "Your faith will not fail while God sustains it; you are not strong enough to fall away while God is resolved to hold you."[5]

Nor Things to Come

When we find ourselves struggling with doubts and fears regarding God's unbreakable love for us, one of the best things we can do is to immerse ourselves in Romans 8. Read J. I. Packer's chapter on Romans 8 in *Knowing God*; read the books on Romans 8 by Ray Ortlund, Octavius Winslow, and Derek Thomas; listen to the sermons of John Piper and read the sermons that Martyn Lloyd-Jones preached from this great chapter.

Romans 8 ends with a confident celebration of God's everlasting love. "For I am sure that neither death nor life, nor angels nor rulers, nor things present nor things to come, nor powers, nor height nor depth, nor anything else in all creation, will be able to separate us from the love of God in Christ Jesus our Lord" (vv. 38–39).

Note that "things to come" (v. 38), a rather all-encompassing category regarding the believer's future, are unable to separate us from God's love.

The proof of God's great love is the giving of his only beloved Son. Verse 32 is extraordinary: "He who did not spare his own Son but gave him up for us all, how will he not also with him graciously give us all things?" God did not spare his Son because that is the only way he could spare us. The Son of God became sin for us and bore the righteous wrath we deserve. And now, what is your future in Christ? God has promised that he will give you all things!

There is irrefutable logic in this verse. It is the logic of the love of God. God has already given us his only Son, which is the greatest gift imaginable because of the infinite love he has for his Son. There is no greater gift; there is nothing more costly to God than to turn his anger upon the Joy of Heaven, to curse the Blessed One, and to cast the Radiance of Glory into darkness—his own Son!

Therefore, if God did the greater thing in his love, he will certainly do lesser things in that same love.

What does it mean that God will give us "all things"? It doesn't mean that he will give you a new car or the house of your dreams. It doesn't mean that all our problems will immediately go away. Rather, it means that God will give us everything we need for spiritual fruitfulness. All that you need to live life faithful to Christ, everything that you need in order to be changed into the image of Christ, he will give.

J. I. Packer explains it this way: "The meaning of 'he will give us all things' can be put thus: one day we shall see that nothing—literally nothing—which could have increased our eternal happiness has been denied us, and that nothing—literally nothing—that could have reduced that happiness has been left with us."[6]

This love is greater than we can fathom! It's no wonder that Paul prays in Ephesians 3 that God would help him to know this love that surpasses knowledge!

One of the most important words in Romans 8:32 is the word "graciously." That this bright future is *graciously* given to us means it is not earned. We so easily fall into thinking that God will give us what we need so long as we work for it or earn it. As long as I don't make mistakes, as long as I try hard to be a super-Christian, as long as I never doubt his love, then God will bless me. But no. He *graciously* gives us all good things.

Kept by Undeserved Love

Your future does not depend on your ability to hold fast to Christ, but on his ability to hold fast to you. Just as we are saved by grace, so we are sustained by grace. Just as we are converted by undeserved love, we are kept by undeserved love.

Charles Spurgeon reminds us of the gracious character of God's love: "Christ did not love you for your good works. They were not the cause of his beginning to love you. So, he does not love you for your good works even now. They are not the cause of his continuing to love you. He loves you because he loves you."[7]

Know today that you are loved as the Lord's treasured possession, now and forever. Rejoice in God's great love, be satisfied in his love, live like you are loved. Octavius Winslow says,

> Our Great Shepherd, Himself slain for the sheep, guides his flock, and has declared that no one shall pluck them out of his hand. We are more than conquerors through his grace who loved us in the very circumstances that threaten to overwhelm. Fear not, then, the darkest cloud, nor the proudest waves, nor the deepest wants—in these very things you shall, through Christ, prove triumphant.[8]

Dark clouds and fierce waves will still come. But here is the question: Are you living in the comfort and security of knowing that the love of God for you is unbreakable and unending? Do you feel loved with the greatest love the world has ever known? This is God's desire for you.

When we fear that our hold on Christ will fail, we must remember his strong hold on us. There is a love that calms and quiets all our fears of the future. There is a love that never dies. We are in the strong and loving hand of Jesus, who promises to keep us in his everlasting love.

Questions for Reflection

1. How does God's love differ from human love?

2. Read Romans 8. According to Romans 8, how does our view of the future change our lives in the present?

Chapter 7

We Will Kiss the Wave

The gospel prepares us for grief and pain

THERE IS A bright tomorrow coming when Christ returns. On that day, we will live in the world we've always longed for—a place of perfect joy, a home where hard times will never come again. In the meantime, it is through many tribulations that we must enter the kingdom of God (Acts 14:22). As we await an imperishable inheritance, we will be, for a little while, grieved by various trials (1 Peter 1:6).

How should we think about the trials that are sure to come?

As Christians, we do not lose heart or shrink back. The grace by which we are saved prepares us for suffering by waging war on fear and unbelief, and by implanting an unshakable hope in our souls.

Penguins are made to endure the cold, anvils are made to endure the hammer, shingles are made to endure the rain, and Christians are made to endure trials. God, in regenerating you, making you a new creation in Christ, has done more to prepare you for suffering than the bravest of unbelievers could ever do for themselves.

The Lord has caused you to be born again to a living hope through the resurrection of Jesus (1 Peter 1:3). He has placed deep within you a love for him as a compass for your soul, a love that turns you to the Lord in all your suffering. The peace of God will be a garrison to your heart and mind when anxieties threaten to overtake you (Philippians 4:6–7). The hope that you have in Christ will not fade, but will only grow in the hour of trial.

The Clouds that You Now Dread

Some of us look ahead and see dark storm clouds looming on the horizon. Remember the words of the hymn writer William Cowper:

> Ye fearful saints, fresh courage take;
> The clouds ye so much dread
> Are big with mercy and shall break
> In blessings on your head.[1]

The only clouds that can come into your life are clouds that are big with mercy. And when those clouds break, they will shower divine blessings on your head.

Courage in the present does not come from believing that future trials will not come, but from knowing that when they do, God will sustain and strengthen us.

Plunder our property, and we will joyfully accept it because we have a better and abiding possession (Hebrews 10:34). Let moth and rust destroy and thieves break in and steal, and our treasures will not be touched (Matthew 6:19–21). Let fiery trials of many kinds come upon us, and we will not be surprised but instead rejoice that we share in Christ's sufferings (1 Peter 4:12–13). Let sudden terror come, and we will not be afraid, for the Lord will be our confidence and our protector (Proverbs 3:25–26). The flood waters rise, but I will not drown. The fires rage, but I will not be burned (Isaiah 43:2).

We know that crisis will come, but the Lord will be with us. Days of weakness and sorrow will come, but they will be days in which the power of God and the joy of the Lord are manifest in us.

David Powlison observes, "In the hands of a loving God, sorrow and suffering become doorways into the greatest and most indestructible joys."[2]

There is an old saying that is popularly attributed to Charles Spurgeon. The origin is uncertain, but the truth is glorious: "I have learned to kiss the wave that throws me against the Rock of Ages."

The worst that the waves of hardship can do is to throw you against the Rock of Ages, work for your good, and prepare for you an eternal weight of glory.

When You Pass through the Waters

The last twenty-seven chapters of the book of Isaiah (chapters 40–66) are a treasure for those facing present or future trials. God enabled the prophet Isaiah to know that great hardship was coming for the people of Israel. Their temple would be destroyed, their land would be taken, and they would spend seventy years in captivity in Babylon. Isaiah foresaw the coming darkness.

Perhaps you look to the future and see difficult days full of tears, loss, sickness, and chronic pain. These chapters of Isaiah were written for you.

Beginning in chapter 40, Isaiah brings a message of comfort and hope to a people overwhelmed with uncertainty and fear regarding the future. God wants his people to know that he has set his affection upon them and that he will be with them, to uphold and deliver them in the hour of trial. He refuses to allow our vision to be limited to trials alone, and calls our attention to himself, the God of all comfort. This is the message God brings in Isaiah 41:9–10:

> "You are my servant,
>   I have chosen you and not cast you off";
> fear not, for I am with you;
>   be not dismayed, for I am your God;

68

I will strengthen you, I will help you,
I will uphold you with my righteous right hand.

Yes, you will suffer, but fear not and be full of good courage. Why? Because, God says, "I have," "I am," and "I will":

- *"I have chosen you."* The Lord has placed his affection upon you. You have been chosen in Christ and belong to God forever.
- *"I am with you"* and *"I am your God."* My feelings may tell me that I am alone, but God says that he is with me. He has not abandoned me; in spite of my sin, he still declares himself to be my God.
- *"I will strengthen, help, and uphold you."* God says, "I will" fourteen times in Isaiah 41. He knows our weakness and he knows every trial we will face. His promise is that he will work on our behalf. He will give you the strength you need for the road ahead.

"I have," "I am," "I will"! Isn't it just like our God, so rich in grace, to care so deeply about persuading us that he will deliver us from a trial that has yet to come? The Lord wants us to know in advance that we should not consider our hardships the end of the story. "For I know the plans I have for you, declares the LORD, plans for welfare and not for evil, to give you a future and a hope" (Jeremiah 29:11).

God sustains his people in every generation, in the times of the prophets and in our own day, by declaring the future plans he has for us in Christ. "I have," "I am," "I will"! These three declarations stand today to banish our fear. And this divine activity must shape our view of whatever hardships may come our way.

"Fear not, for I have redeemed you;
I have called you by name, you are mine.

When you pass through the waters, I will be with you;
  and through the rivers, they shall not overwhelm
    you;
when you walk through the fire you shall not be burned,
  and the flame shall not consume you." (Isaiah
    43:1–2)

He Will Hold Me Fast

On March 12, 2017, exactly nine months after Aggie's cancer diagnosis, Meghan and I stood in front of our church family to express our gratitude and to testify to the sustaining grace of God through the most difficult trial we have known. I held Aggie while Meghan did the talking. Aggie had only been able to make it to church a couple of times since her diagnosis, so it was special to have her there.

One of the most powerful ways we experienced God's grace was through the love and support that came through our church. They provided countless meals, stayed with Aggie on Sunday mornings so Meghan could attend church, watched our kids, cleaned our house, helped with grocery shopping, visited us in the hospital, prayed for us, and much more.

That Sunday morning, Meghan read two journal entries to the church, to testify to the way Christ had held her fast in the midst of great sorrow. One journal entry was written two weeks after Aggie's diagnosis. The extended grief and trauma that Meghan experienced during those months was overwhelming.

It was in that place of deep sorrow that she held on to the truth that Christ was holding on to her. She had a sense that God was telling her that her testimony would be that she is weak and fearful, but Christ is holding her fast. This is what Meghan wrote on June 26, 2016:

Tonight is the second time in two weeks that I am sleeping in my own bed. But every time I come home and Aggie and Jared are not with me, my heart is overwhelmed with sorrow. Tucking Juliet and Lily into bed and seeing Aggie's empty crib is just so sad; crawling into bed without Jared beside me is just so sad.

And I can wonder if life over the next two years will always have at least a shadow of sadness in it . . . I can wonder if we will ever have moments of laughter and joy and light-heartedness.

My heart is truly overwhelmed with sorrow and I can't think about the future without fear and sorrow. But my Savior knows overwhelming sorrow. And I do know that Christ will hold me fast. And I know that His love for all of us is deeper, stronger, and more tender than I can comprehend.

And so I trust. I cry, but I trust . . . my heart aches, but I trust . . . I tremble, but I trust . . . my foot slips, but I trust because Christ will hold me fast.

Nearly eight months later, on January 9, 2017, this is what she wrote:

The past few days I've been struck by how much joy Aggie brings to our whole family. She is a joyful little girl and she spreads her joy wherever she goes!

As I've thought about this, I've been reminded of the thoughts and fears that I had those early days of Aggie's cancer diagnosis. I feared that our family would no longer have light moments that are full of laughter . . . I thought the heaviness and darkness of childhood cancer would be there all the time, overshadowing everything and stamping out the laughter and light . . . I just couldn't imagine a time of not feeling agonizingly sad.

But I realized this morning that that is something I forgot I felt . . . it's a distant memory. The Lord has been kind and gracious and answered so many prayers. He has poured out grace on Aggie and given her a resilient, joyful spirit and that in turn blesses our whole family. It's truly a thing to behold: to see this little girl with her sweet, little bald head enjoying life . . . even with her current limitations.

The Lord knew my fears and he heard my cries for help and before I even realized it, he answered those prayers and quieted those fears. Thank you, Lord! And what I never expected is that he has given us a deeper joy in the everyday than we had before cancer because we take fewer things for granted. He has given us more than I asked or imagined—not just preserving joy and light and laughter, but actually deepening it and increasing it even in the presence of sorrow. Christ indeed is holding us fast.

Meghan concluded her comments to the church with these words: "And so I bear testimony this morning that in my own strength I'm a weak and fearful mom, but Christ is holding me fast . . . he has not left me on my own for a moment. He has had me face one of my worst nightmares as a mom and in that place he has proved himself over and over. All my hope is in him."

Great Truths for Future Trials

It is not the will of God for us to face suffering with stoicism or fatalism. But God's Word arms us with the truths we need to face any hardships that come our way with confidence in Christ. What are the truths that prepare us for future sorrows?

God watches over us with fatherly care. Our comfort is in knowing that nothing will befall us apart from our Father's good and sovereign purpose. The opening Question and Answer in *The Heidelberg Catechism*, regarding our only comfort in life and death, says that Christ "watches over me in such a way that not a hair can fall from my head without the will of my Father in heaven: in fact, all things must work together for my salvation."[3]

Our suffering is always appointed, never accidental. John Calvin says that nothing is more useful than a knowledge of the doctrine of God's providence.[4] He says that the providence of God means that nothing happens but what God has knowingly and willingly decreed.[5] This is good news for God's children. "Sacred is the security which reclines on his providence."[6] You can experience this security today.

In the wisdom of God, the divine purposes now hidden will one day be revealed. Presently there are mysteries in the providence of God. But in the future, we will see the goal of our present experience. This infuses purpose into all our struggles and sorrows. The parts of our lives that presently seem meaningless will one day be revealed as full of meaning.

We are like Joseph in the book of Genesis. In the present, we are hated, mistreated, lonely, and falsely accused. But a day is coming, as it came for Joseph, when God's good purposes will be revealed. We will confess with our mouths and see with eyes of faith that even where evil was done against us, God meant it all for our good (Genesis 50:20).

Charles Spurgeon says,

> The day will come when you will be astonished that there was order in your life when you thought it all confusion. You will be astonished that there was love and you thought it unkindness, that there was gentleness and you thought it severity, that there was wisdom when you were wicked enough to impugn God's righteousness.[7]

Entrusting ourselves to the wisdom of God means we resolve that no matter what comes our way, we will declare to the Lord, "You are good and do good" (Psalm 119:68). We will entrust our lives to his good purposes for us and know that he intends this for good.

The Lord is your protector. Psalm 91 is a celebration of God's protection in the midst of unknown future hardships. "Because you have made the LORD your dwelling place—the Most High, who is my refuge—no evil shall be allowed to befall you, no plague come near your tent" (91:9–10).

If I did not have the certainty of God's protection all my days, I would panic over the unknown and despair in the darkness. But the Lord is my refuge and my fortress (91:2), my guardian and my deliverer. His faithfulness is a shield and a buckler (91:4).

What does God's promised protection mean? It means that the Lord will protect you from divine wrath, he will sustain your faith, he will keep you from stumbling, he will guard your soul, he will keep you safe from the Evil One and thwart the purposes of all your enemies. When you call to him, he will answer you and rescue you. "I will be with him in trouble" (91:15).

Therefore, "you will not fear the terror of the night, nor the arrow that flies by day" (91:5). We will tread on lions and trample the serpent under our feet (91:13). Christ is our mighty protector, and by his power we will look in triumph upon our enemies (Psalm 59:10).

God uses suffering to make us more like Christ. Isaiah 48:10 says, "Behold, I have refined you, but not as silver; I have tried you in the furnace of affliction." God is refining us, maturing us, and making us more like Christ. In suffering he often works in us in ways we are unaware, growing us in ways we would never grow merely through our own effort.

Our afflictions produce eternal glory. The apostle Paul knew imprisonment and shipwrecks, beatings and stonings, hunger and thirst, weariness and sorrow, pain and suffering (2 Corinthians 11:23–28). Yet in all his afflictions he knew the truth of 2 Corinthians 4:17: "For this light momentary affliction is preparing for us an eternal weight of glory beyond all comparison."

The deeper our suffering, the greater our hope. Trials are God's way of detaching our hearts from this world, deepening our longing for heaven. "We rejoice in our sufferings, knowing that suffering produces endurance, and endurance produces character, and character produces hope" (Romans 5:3–4).

The God of all comfort will comfort us in all our sorrows. Wherever suffering takes you, God's comfort will find you. He is "the Father of mercies and God of all comfort, who comforts us in all our affliction" (2 Corinthians 1:3–4). Isaiah 51:3 says, "For the LORD comforts Zion; he comforts all her waste places and makes her wilderness like Eden, her desert like the garden of the LORD; joy and gladness will be found in her, thanksgiving and the voice of song." The more our earthly comforts are lost, the deeper our comforts in the love of God.

Suffering equips us to minister God's comfort to others. Second Corinthians 1:4 says that the reason God comforts us in affliction is "so that we may be able to comfort those who are in any affliction, with the comfort with which we ourselves are comforted by God."

All things are working together for our good. Romans 8:28 is true, and just imagine the confidence we would have if we could live like it's true. "And we know that for those who love God all things work together for good, for those who are called according to his purpose."

Nothing can come your way except those things that will be to your ultimate benefit. You cannot remove yourself from the path of divine beneficence. We weary ourselves with anxiety, even while all things continue to conspire for our good. For those in Christ, the worst our enemies can do is to contribute unknowingly to the fulfillment of God's good plans for us.

Trials magnify the faithfulness of God to us. The trials of life are those places where the faithfulness of God is loudly declared. Every danger and every sorrow magnifies the glory of God's sustaining grace. There he proves his protection and demonstrates his power.

God will richly reward our steadfastness in suffering. In the book of James, God instructs us to count it all joy when we meet trials of various kinds (1:2). This is because we know the greater steadfastness, maturity, and faith God is producing in us through trials (1:3–4), and the reward that comes to those who endure hardship by the power of God. "Blessed is the man who remains steadfast under trial, for when he has stood the test he will receive the crown of life, which God has promised to those who love him" (1:12).

God uses suffering to teach us about himself. Many of us can testify, "Before I was afflicted I went astray, but now I keep your word" (Psalm 119:67). Therefore, "It is good for me that I was afflicted, that I might learn your statutes" (Psalm 119:71).

The cross of Christ gives essential perspective in our suffering. What if the darkest hour of history could become the moment of greatest glory? What if the death of Christ and the apparent triumph of evil could become the praise of heaven and the victory of God? This is exactly what God has done.

The cross of Christ is the guarantee that God brings joy out of sorrow and life out of death. If God gave his Son for us, he is forever for us and his love has been proven once for all. John Stott observes, "We have to learn to climb the hill called Calvary, and from that vantage-ground survey all life's tragedies. The cross does not solve the problem of suffering, but it supplies the essential perspective from which to look at it."[8]

If you knew the story God is writing, you wouldn't despise this present chapter or fear what might happen in the next.

All of the suffering of God's people will one day end. The gospel teaches us to look beyond a life of sorrow to an eternity of joy. Present groaning will soon give way to future glorification. The death and resurrection of Christ guarantee a future in which God himself will wipe every tear from our eyes. There will be no mourning, no crying, and no pain, for these belong to the former things that will pass away (Revelation 21:4).

What more can God say?! He has loved us, he is with us, he will strengthen and uphold us. In this life, sorrows will come. I must allow the good news of what Christ has done to prepare me for suffering. I will entrust myself now and forever to the goodness of God. I will weep and lament and long for the age to come.

And until that day, I will also rejoice in suffering, and kiss every wave that throws me against the Rock of Ages.

Questions for Reflection

1. What difficult situation have you gone through that you can now look back on and see how God helped and sustained you?

2. Which of the "Great Truths for Future Trials" shared in the last part of this chapter is most encouraging and timely for you?

Chapter 8

For Parents Who Worry

Love your kids by laughing at the days to come

PROVERBS 31 PROVIDES a familiar portrait of a life marked by virtue, maturity, and wisdom. The portrait is not an outline of required activities for every woman, but a description of wisdom in action. It is not intended to discourage, but to inspire.

One of the most compelling features of the woman described in Proverbs 31 is her view of the future in relation to her household. There is something here for all parents, whether mothers or fathers, to emulate. She does not fear what change might bring to her family: "She is not afraid of snow for her household" (31:21). She is so strong and dignified, it's as if these qualities are the clothes she wears: "Strength and dignity are her clothing, and she laughs at the time to come" (31:25). Her view of the future is not marked by worry or fear, but by a joyful trust in the Lord. She looks at the future, and she laughs.

While this chapter is written with parents directly in view, my hope is that it will also help those who are not parents but may worry about someone they love.

Common Parental Fears

No parent wants to be clothed with fear and anxiety. But we often find that we lack confidence in Christ for the future of our family. We raise our children under the burden of worst-case scenarios, and our parenting is dominated by the tyranny of "What if . . . ?"

Parental fears are familiar and common to us all:

- Fear of negative influences. *What if bad company leads our children astray?*
- Fear that we are ruining our kids. *What if we are depriving our kids of the nurture, training, and opportunities they need to reach their potential?*
- Fear of embarrassing our family. *What if they become a source of shame?*
- Fear that they will not be normal. *What if they are not like other kids, or don't fit in socially?*
- Fear of physical or emotional harm. *What if they have an accident or injury or disease, or someone hurts them?*
- Fear that they will not live for Christ. *What if they deny the gospel, rebel against Christ, and pursue a life of folly and sin?*

Our heavenly Father invites us to entrust our children to his care, to remember the power of his gospel as we train them, to cease from anxiety-producing self-reliance, and to love our children by walking in the joy of hope. Only as we learn the power and love of Christ toward us and our children can we laugh at the days to come.

"Do Not Fear, Only Believe"

In the book of Mark, there are thirteen individuals who are minor characters, each facing a distinct trouble in a fallen world. These characters close the distance between the first-century world and our own. Each of these men and women come to Jesus for help, and Jesus, full of mercy, meets them in their distress.

Among them is a synagogue official named Jairus, whose twelve-year-old daughter is dying and then dead. Mark 5 tells the story of this father and the fear he faces.

When Jairus first saw Jesus, he fell at his feet, desperately imploring him. "My little daughter is at the point of death" (Mark 5:23). Jesus agreed to go with him. Along the way, someone from Jairus's house came and informed him that his daughter was dead. Jesus overheard this and spoke words of hope to Jairus: "Do not fear, only believe" (5:36).

Faith is the solution to fear, including the fears we have regarding our children. In every situation, parents are called to a practical trust in the Lord.

When Jesus arrived, he directed the crowd to leave the house, and went with Jairus and his wife to see their daughter. Jesus drew near and took the hand of this little girl in his own hand. Then came the words of life: *Talitha cumi*. "Little girl, I say to you, arise."

Some of us know what it's like to experience a daughter at death's door. In one way or another, every parent knows what it's like to fear for the well-being of a dearly loved child.

Here is what I've learned from the story of Jairus's daughter: First, *we should never forget that Jesus loves our kids even more than we do*. The attention Jesus gave to this child is consistent with his affectionate disposition toward other children. He said, "Let the children come to me" (Mark 10:14), and "he took them in his arms and blessed them, laying his hands on them" (10:16).

God knows and personally loves each one of your children. He has made them just as they are. And he has sovereignly placed them in your home so that they will learn about him and his salvation. It is proof of the Lord's kindness to your children and evidence of his pursuit of them.

Second, *Jesus is eager to meet parents in moments of distress*. When Jairus came to Jesus in his moment of need, Jesus did not turn him away. We too can go to Jesus, fall at his feet, and earnestly implore him to help our children. Whether their needs are physical or spiritual, Jesus enters our distress and involves himself in our cares, because we are greatly loved by him.

Third, *Jesus can do for our children what we cannot do*. Only God can bring a child from death to life. This means that our children's greatest need—salvation from sin and death—is beyond our ability to provide.

There should be something of Jairus's desperation and dependence that marks our parenting. Go to Jesus on behalf of your children. Turn your worries about your kids into prayers for your kids. Our Father in heaven will hear our prayers. Cast your cares upon the Lord, knowing that he cares for you. "Do not be anxious about anything, but in everything by prayer and supplication with thanksgiving let your requests be made known to God. And the peace of God, which surpasses all understanding, will guard your hearts and your minds in Christ Jesus" (Philippians 4:6–7).

God's work in the lives of our children is in no way limited by our shortcomings. We are often aware of the limitations we bring to the parenting task. Our strength fails us, our wisdom falters, our example comes up short. I do not want to downplay the importance of parental faithfulness, yet we must insist that the determining factor in the lives of our children is the grace and power of God.

Fourth, *Jesus gives us faith to do all he calls us to do*. He not only gives the command to walk in faith and to resist fear, he acts in a way that draws forth our trust. He puts his power, his love, and his wisdom on display in our lives. Jesus has proven his goodness once for all in the death he died. The cross is a statement that God is for you and God is with you. Anxious parenting is the result of being more aware of our weakness than God's power, more aware of sin than grace, more aware of human folly than divine wisdom, more aware of rebellion than rescue, more aware of death than life.

Prodigals and the Power of Christ

I regret that my teen years were spent living for myself. One of the first things you would have noticed when you walked into the church I attended growing up was the disrespectful pastor's kid in the front row, who sat bored and lifeless during the entire service, including the sermon. That was me.

There was a three-year period of my life—from when I was fourteen to when I was sixteen—when my parents thought they had lost me for good. And they *had* lost me, in the sense that they no longer had any control over my behavior and I didn't care about obeying them or obeying God.

I defined God on my own terms, and he became a god who didn't have opinions about how I lived. I withdrew from my parents. The attitude that I adopted toward others was, "I'll leave you alone and you leave me alone. I'm not going to ask anything from you, and all I want is for you to return the favor."

The world had a strong pull on my heart, and I started doing things behind my parents' backs. I told my parents I didn't care about having regrets and I even told them that I wanted to have regrets. In every conversation with my parents, my goal was to provoke my dad to anger and to make my mom cry. Unfortunately, I was pretty good at both of these things.

In February of 1996, when I was in tenth grade, I started dating a girl who was not a Christian. My relationship with Meghan (now my wife) became serious. I hid it from my parents for as long as I could. When they eventually found out, I told them things weren't going to change.

In short, I was an enemy of God. I was opposed to him in my sin and he was justly opposed to me in his holiness.

I thank God that my parents didn't give up on me. More importantly, God didn't give up on me. A few years later, God worked in my life through conversations my parents initiated with me and through the prayers of many people in our church. I became convinced of my sin and folly. I knew I was failing to honor my parents, and failing to honor God in my relationship with Meghan. By the power of the risen Christ, my eyes were opened up to see God's grace in Christ for the first time. The God who said, "Let light shine out of darkness," had shone in my heart to give the light of the knowledge of the glory of God in the face of Jesus Christ (2 Corinthians 4:6).

Regeneration has a way of changing things. The old was gone, the new had come. I was a new creation, with new priorities and passions. The prodigal had come home.

No Hopeless Cases

In Luke 15, the Prodigal Son who wandered so far from home and ran so far from grace found, as many prodigals have, that his rebellion was not the end of the story. There is more grace in Christ than there is sin in the greatest of prodigals, and therefore, we never lose hope.

There is a mighty Savior who finds the lost. There is a mighty Savior who brings the dead back to life. This mighty Savior laid down his life and is alive today, seeking and saving the lost. There are prodigals like me whose stories testify that there are no hopeless cases.

John Newton was raised in a Christian home. His mother taught him God's Word and hymns and catechized him at a young age. He ran off and joined the Royal Navy and gained a reputation for his complete lack of morality. But God goes where parents cannot go and he is the God who can do things that we as parents cannot do in the lives of our children. One day when Newton was out at sea, God sent a storm that was used to convert Newton. He went on to be a faithful Christian, a skilled pastor, and an influential hymn writer. The grace he celebrated he knew from experience: "Amazing grace, how sweet the sound, that saved a wretch like me."

Christian parents have reason for great confidence. It's not because we have a guarantee that our children will be saved. When the Lord says, "Train up a child in the way he should go; even when he is old he will not depart from it" (Proverbs 22:6), it is not an absolute promise but a general observation of how things most often work in God's world.

Therefore, we cannot give parents a settled guarantee that their children will turn to Christ. But we can give the truth that the gospel is more powerful than we know, and has a way of taking root and bearing fruit in spite of parental weaknesses and youthful rebellion. If Christ has risen, and if Christ reigns with power and love, there are no hopeless cases.

Grace Is Greater

Sometimes as parents we think, "But my kids seem strongly inclined toward sin." In those moments, we must remember that God is even more strongly inclined toward grace.

Satan wants us to live with a constant sense of guilt regarding our parenting failures. God wants us to live and parent in the confidence of his grace.

Maybe you have fears because you are a single parent, or because your spouse is an unbeliever or is a believer but not proactive in training your children. You feel that your situation is not "ideal." And there may be a sense in which that is true.

But I've noticed that Christians and churches are at times so committed to celebrating the ideal family situation that we fail to celebrate the grace that triumphs in the midst of brokenness, sin, and loss and in situations we don't consider ideal. Our hope is not in what we consider ideal, but in the true ideal of the good and sovereign plan God has for us.

The nuclear family is a great blessing, but it is a lousy savior. We must repent of the idolatry and self-reliance of a family-centric faith, and acknowledge our tendency to misplace our confidence. Even a faithful, two-parent, Christian home can never meet a child's greatest need, which is salvation from sin and death. Our hope is not an unbroken family existence; our hope is a Savior who works in the midst of brokenness.

This needs to be emphasized for single parents: The gospel is powerful to supply what is lacking when there is only one parent in the picture. The idea that your children are destined to failure, or even that they are more likely to fail because they lack both parents, is not a thought born of the Spirit of God. It is born of the Enemy. It is a lie.

Someone says, "Well, the statistics show that children with only one parent are less likely to flourish." But since when is our faith governed by statistics? What did the statistics say about a dead man rising from the grave on the third day? What did the statistics say about the probability of any of us being rescued from the judgment we deserve?

In fact, single parents need to know that they are the object of the Father's special care. Leif Enger's novel, *Peace Like a River*, is a story that centers around a single-parent father named Jeremiah Land. He supports his three children by working as a school janitor. At one point, Enger says regarding Jeremiah's kids, "The small and the vulnerable own a protection great enough, if you could but see it, to melt you into jelly. Beware those who reside beneath the shadow of the Wings."[1]

Exodus 22:22–24 says, "You shall not mistreat any widow or fatherless child. If you do mistreat them, and they cry out to me, I will surely hear their cry, and my wrath will burn." That command and warning is from the heart of the eternal God. "Beware those who reside beneath the shadow of the Wings." Single parents, God is able to care for you and your children without another parent in the picture. Rather than viewing things as stacked against you and your kids, realize that God is for you and has pledged his special care to you.

How to Really Bless Your Kids

The goal of this chapter has been to remind parents of the reasons they have for confidence regarding their children. Not only is the presence of faith pleasing to God, it is also one of the best things you can give your children.

Fear will be a burden to our souls and will exasperate our children (Ephesians 6:4) because we are seeking to control the uncontrollable. Parental fear robs us of the peace and joy we have in Christ, which is what our kids most need to see in us.

The most important thing you can do for your kids is to delight your soul in the Lord, trust in his goodness, embrace his sovereignty, and face the future with faith. The gospel frees us to model the difference that grace makes. Grace means that we are not called to model perfect parenting, but can model what it looks like to need a Savior. Grace means we don't need to fear that God is going to punish us for our parental failures. Grace means that God's love for us is settled, so that nothing can steal our joy in Christ. Grace means that your kids are not now, and never will be, beyond the reach of God's strong arm.

By the power of grace, do not be afraid. Clothe yourself with dignity and strength. Laugh at the days to come.

Questions for Reflection

1. If you are a parent, what is a common fear you face related to parenting? If you are not a parent, is there a common fear you face about someone you love?

2. What reasons do Christian parents have to raise their kids with confidence?

Chapter 9

A Culture of Panic

The triumph of hope in the midst of cultural crisis

WHEN JOHN PERKINS was sixteen years old, his older brother Clyde was shot and killed by a deputy marshal. It happened while Clyde was waiting to enter a movie theater. He stood in line at the side entrance that African-Americans were forced to use, which led to the segregated section of the theater where African-Americans had to sit. John's older brother died in his arms that night.

John Perkins became a Christian in his twenties and went on to become a leader in the civil rights movement. To this day he continues to be a powerful voice for justice, racial reconciliation, and community development. At one point he moved to California, where he found job opportunities and a much easier life. But God called him to return to Mississippi with the message of Christ to work for justice there.

In the early 1970s, Perkins was brutally beaten, mocked, and physically tortured by the sheriff and state police. They knocked him unconscious, and when he would come to, he was called racist names and forced to mop up all of his blood. Ethnic-based police brutality led to ethnic-based injustice from a corrupt legal system.

But the life of John Perkins is a life that adorns the gospel of Jesus Christ with mercy and forgiveness. He believes that the sound of love is powerful to drown out the sound of hatred. He believes in the triumph of hope in the chaos of cultural crisis and injustice. And his life can only be explained by the fact that Christ took hold of him.[1]

How should Christians respond to cultural decline, moral decay, and distressing social issues? Not with hopelessness or withdrawal. Not with triumphalism, panic, or despair. We respond with hope.

The message of Christ's kingdom does not tell us only about our personal future. It includes a message of social reordering and gives us a hope-filled vision of where society and history are ultimately headed.

The advance of the kingdom is certain. One day, all things will be placed under the feet of King Jesus. As the Southern Baptist theologian and preacher Russell Moore says, "God's kingdom triumph is proven not by our electoral success or our cultural influence. . . . Our triumph is proven in the resurrection of the world's rightful ruler."[2]

Good News about Injustice

Gary Haugen is no stranger to the evils and injustices that plague our world. Haugen is a Christian who spent years working as a trial attorney in the civil rights division of the U. S. Department of Justice. In 1994, he became the founder and president of International Justice Mission (IJM), a global human rights agency that protects the poor, rescues victims, strengthens justice systems, addresses social and structural injustices, and works tirelessly for the cause of mercy.

Haugen wrote a book called *Good News about Injustice* presenting the biblical teaching about the importance of seeking justice. He says that according to IJM's research and observations, the most common or prevalent injustices in the world today include:

- Cruel child labor
- Child prostitution

- Abusive and corrupt police
- Extortion
- Murder
- Genocide
- Organized racial violence
- Public justice corruption
- State-supported discrimination of ethnic minorities
- Religious persecution
- Torture
- Slavery

Our hearts break when we consider the darkness that fills the earth. Throughout history and to this day, we can hear the world groaning under the effects of the fall. Pornography is an industry. Protests turn violent. Moral relativism abounds. Sexual ethics and the institution of marriage have been abandoned. There are threats to the freedom of religion. The problem of mass incarceration continues to grow. The unborn continue to be slaughtered. There is talk of war. Brash and shameless leaders are elected to govern nations. Fear and hatred surround us.

We cry, "How long, O LORD?" (Psalm 13:1).

Injustice, violence, and oppression are the result of the fall. The pervasive effects of the fall mean that both individuals and systems are broken. There are personal and social aspects to the justice we desire.

Russell Moore says, "The Bible shows us from the beginning that the scope of the curse is holistic in its destruction—personal, cosmic, social, vocational (Genesis 3–11), and the Bible shows us in the end that the gospel is holistic in its restoration—personal, cosmic, social, vocational (Revelation 21–22)."[3] In other words, we need holistic redemption because the world is holistically messed up.

Christians do not lose heart, because God has equipped us in his Word of truth with an understanding of evil. We have the categories of truth needed to respond with love, justice, and hope. We know that the world is fallen, so we are not surprised by the millions of people who suffer great injustices. "If you see in a province the oppression of the poor and the violation of justice and righteousness, do not be amazed at the matter" (Ecclesiastes 5:8).

We reject the utopian vision of the gradual betterment of humanity. We do not believe that our efforts will eradicate all injustice and usher in worldwide peace. Gary Haugen writes, "We are not caught up in a Pollyanna-like dream of bringing heaven to earth and abolishing injustice. On the contrary, we know that an ocean of oppression will pound humanity until he whom even the wind and waves obey shall command the storm to cease (Matthew 8:27)."[4]

We also know, as Haugen says, that "the battle against oppression stands or falls on the battlefield of hope."[5] Our great hope is that the gospel holds out the guarantee of a better future in Christ. The kingdom of God has come and will be consummated when King Jesus returns. We believe the good news that all things will be reconciled under Christ, all tears will be wiped from our eyes, all sorrow, suffering, and injustice will end, and therefore we have a mighty hope.

The Panic of Impoverished Theology

Christian cultural engagement has not always emitted the aroma of hope. Too often, our tone has been alarmist, apocalyptic, and abrasive.

A spokesperson for the religious right once made a terribly misinformed statement and claimed that what liberal America is now doing to evangelical Christians is just like what Nazi Germany did to the Jews. On the other end of the political spectrum, Christians with a more liberal social agenda are generally no better, often operating with a misplaced hope in humanity's ability to fashion a just and equitable world apart from Christ and his return. The result is a tone of outrage on all sides.

This panic and hysteria is not only bad for politics, it is a poor representation of the Christian faith. Cultural panic is the result of an impoverished theology of the kingdom of God. We too easily lose sight of the kingdom that is coming, and when that happens, we exchange our future hope for the idol of political power.

Just as God's people have done throughout history, many Christians today have a tendency to trust in power, military might, and getting the "right" public officials in place. This results in fearful and alarmist tones, the vilification of political opponents, and the fragile joy that rises and falls depending on whether or not our candidate wins.

There is a better way. My trust is not in our president. My trust is not in the economy. My trust is not in the moral direction of our culture. "Some trust in chariots and some in horses, but we trust in the name of the LORD our God. They collapse and fall, but we rise and stand upright" (Psalm 20:7–8).

Our ability to honor Christ as believers is never contingent upon our possession of political power. In fact, sometimes the way we respond when we don't get what we hoped for politically is our most powerful witness in the public square. The darker the days, the brighter our hope will shine. The greater the anxieties of our world, the more powerful our witness to Christ will be.

Carl Henry once noted, "The early church didn't say, 'Look what the world is coming to!' They said, 'Look what has come into the world!'"[6]

I remember reading about Chicken Little at my grandma's house. Chicken Little is an old folk tale about the perils of panic and the value of courage. The story centers on a chicken who thinks the world is coming to an end when an acorn falls on his head. The chicken runs around telling all his friends that the sky is falling, sending everyone into mass hysteria. The chicken decides to travel to the king to inform him that the sky is falling. In the end, all the animals who believe and follow the chicken are eaten by a fox.

Christians should never take a Chicken Little approach to cultural engagement. Kevin DeYoung says, "The sky is not falling, and it won't fall until Jesus falls from it first."[7]

We do well to always remember that *hope has a tone*. A panicked and fearful tone is inconsistent with the hope we profess. Our hope is not in this life. We have set our hope fully on the grace that will be brought to us at the return of Christ (1 Peter 1:13). Setting our hope fully on that heavenly kingdom changes the way we relate to the kingdom of this world.

I am not advocating passivity. I am advocating a healthy dose of the sovereignty of God over human history, which fills our social engagement with unshakable confidence, hope, and joy.

Russell Moore models this hope in his life and witness, and articulates it powerfully in his book *Onward*:

> The kingdom's advance is set in motion by the Galilean march out of the graveyard. We should then be the last people on earth to skulk back in fear or apathy. And we ought also be the last people on earth to uncritically laud any political leader or movement as though this is what we've been waiting for. We need leaders and allies, but we do not need a Messiah. That job is filled, and he's feeling fine. We are neither irrationally exuberant, nor fearfully isolated. We recognize that from Golgotha to Armageddon, there will be tumult—in our cultures, in our communities, and in our own psyches. We groan against this, and work to hold back the consequences of the curse. But we do not despair, as those who are the losers in history might. We are the future kings and queens of the universe.[8]

The gospel gives us a new way of seeing the world. God empowers us in Christ to engage culture with the enthusiasm and perseverance that hope gives. The certainty of God's victory is our peace.

Let Justice Roll Down

Andrew Peterson wrote a beautiful series of books called *The Wingfeather Saga*. One of the characters, a boy named Janner Wingfeather, finds himself enslaved in a dark and terrible place called the Fork Factory, where many stolen children were enslaved and used to make weapons and other items. Many of the children had spent years there in darkness and misery. The children are treated with cruelty. They are referred to as "tools" and their names are not used. They never looked each other in the eyes; they were worn down and had lost all hope.

The series tells the story of those children finally being set free. The evil Overseer who runs the factory is defeated and the children are led into safety and beams of sunlight. "The children held their hands up to the light as if it were the first time they'd ever seen it. The moment of awe was quickly broken, however, by squeals of delight and celebration. The children of the Fork Factory danced and ran and tumbled across the floor. They found water in a trough against the wall and splashed it on their faces, rubbing the soot away and meeting each other, in a way, for the very first time."[9]

We can be just like these children and forget that the sunlight is waiting. The injustice that covers our land will not last forever. God has promised that because of Christ, all injustice will one day end.

There may be times in this world when, like Israel, we weary God with our complaints and say, "Where is the God of justice?" (Malachi 2:17). But the cross of Christ, the kingdom of God, and the love of our Father speak a better word. We will not lose heart, for we know that the victory belongs to the Lord. His kingdom will be fully and eternally established.

Isaiah 9 says that the promised Savior would bring a new government over which he reigns as Prince of Peace. "Of the increase of his government and of peace there will be no end, on the throne of David and over his kingdom, to establish it and to uphold it with justice and with righteousness from this time forth and forevermore. The zeal of the LORD of hosts will do this" (9:7).

Your Kingdom Come

The kingdom of God refers to Christ's sovereign rule and reign. His kingdom is present and it is future. It is both *already* and *not yet*. We have already entered the kingdom, yet one day the kingdom will fully come and bring all the blessings of God's reign to all the earth. Then Habakkuk 2:14 will come to pass: "For the earth will be filled with the knowledge of the glory of the LORD as the waters cover the sea."

Our hope is not set on this age, because we know the perfection and fullness of the kingdom will only arrive in the age to come, when Christ returns. We are not disillusioned or discouraged, because we never expected the consummation of the kingdom in this present evil age.

Kingdom hope does not bring an end to lament, but sets lament into hope-filled action. Christians are part of the great resistance. We know that the world is not as it should be, and so we pray, lament, create beauty, do good, and care for the needy as acts of hope-filled protest, witnessing to a kingdom that is sure to come.

The biblical teaching is not that we leave this world for another, but that one age gives way to another. We pray, "Your kingdom come" (Matthew 6:10), and that prayer will be answered when Christ our King returns in glory. Every time we pray for God's kingdom to come, we are praying, whether we realize it or not, for the future of justice, ethics, government, and culture. When God's kingdom fully comes, it will be the end of all injustice, immorality, unethical behavior, corrupt and self-serving governments, and fallen aspects of culture.

God has not forgotten the injustices of the world. He sees, he cares, and he will act. God is determined to bring all evil to an end. And his fierce commitment to justice is the ground for our unshakable hope.

Second Thessalonians 1:6–9 says that God will consider it just to repay with affliction those who afflict you, and when Christ returns he will inflict vengeance on those who reject the gospel. "They will suffer the punishment of eternal destruction, away from the presence of the Lord and from the glory of his might" (v. 9).

The reality of eternal judgment from a holy God will not dampen our eternal joy. Even as God judges unrepentant sinners, his justice will be displayed, his faithfulness will be proven, and his name will be glorified. In some mysterious way that we cannot fully comprehend in this life, the just judgments of God will eternally deepen our joy in him.

The return of Christ will be a public demonstration of his glory and a celebration of the consummation of his rule. Christ will return on a white horse, full of power, and justice will roll down. The Lord will judge those who perpetuate oppression, and justice will roll down. The God of peace will crush Satan under your feet, and justice will roll down. The captive children will hold their hands to the light, they will dance and run, and justice will roll down. God's kingdom will come, and justice will roll down.

What the World Will Be

Christians know that history is going somewhere—it is not a random series of events, but has a God-appointed goal. Charles Spurgeon says, "The events of history march as a victorious legion under a skillful leader."[10] What will the world one day be?

A world of love. Presently, even the church of Christ fails to love as we ought. This is true of our love for God and our love for each other. But in the age to come, we will clearly apprehend the love of Christ for us, and this will create an enjoyment of Christ and each other that is unlike anything we have known. Hatred, strife, impatience, irritability, and violence will be no more, and we will dwell together in a world of perfect love.

A world of peace. One day wars and racism and conflict will end. John Perkins said that one goal of the gospel is to burn through racial and social barriers. "Only the power of Christ's crucifixion on the cross and the glory of His resurrection can heal the deep racial wounds in both black and white people in America."[11] The day is coming when people from every ethnicity will dwell in perfect peace, and every racial wound will be healed by the power of the gospel.

A world of justice. There will be equity for those who have known poverty, marginalization, and oppression. Those who mourn will be comforted and the meek shall inherit the earth (Matthew 5:4–5).

The Russian novelist Fyodor Dostoyevsky in *The Brothers Karamazov* writes,

> I believe like a child that suffering will be healed and made up for, that all the humiliating absurdity of human contradictions will vanish like a pitiful mirage. In the world's finale, at the moment of eternal harmony, something so precious will come to pass that it will suffice. It will comfort all resentments. It will atone for all the crimes, for all the blood that has been shed, that it will make it not only possible to forgive but to justify everything that happens.[12]

A world of beauty. Everything that is ugly and vile will pass away, and the world will be full of God-honoring pleasure, creativity, attraction, and artistry.

A world of abundance. The prophet Isaiah says that this new world will be rich and vibrant: "And he will give rain for the seed with which you sow the ground, and bread, the produce of the ground, which will be rich and plenteous. In that day your livestock will graze in large pastures. . . . And on every lofty mountain and every high hill there will be brooks running with water" (30:23–25).

A world of safety. Isaiah 11:6–9 says that the predatory animals will be changed, no longer able to harm other animals or us.

> The wolf shall dwell with the lamb, and the leopard shall lie down with the young goat, and the calf and the lion and the fattened calf together; and a little child shall lead them. The cow and the bear shall graze; their young shall lie down together; and the lion shall eat straw like the ox. The nursing child shall play over the hole of the cobra, and the weaned child shall put his hand on the adder's den. They shall not hurt or destroy in all my holy mountain; for the earth shall be full of the knowledge of the LORD as the waters cover the sea.

A world of health. No doctors and nurses, no hospitals, no chemotherapy, no Band-Aids, no medicine of any kind. Sickness and disease will be no more.

A world of praise. Depression, sorrow, and unbelief will be gone. We will fall face-down before the once-slain, now-standing Lamb of God, and with hearts of wonder we will worship him and declare him worthy of eternal praise. We will join with all the living creatures, the elders, and the great multitude of angels in heaven, lifting our voices in shouts of joy: "To him who sits on the throne and to the Lamb be blessing and honor and glory and might forever and ever!" (Revelation 5:13).

Until that day, our God is a fortress, a tower of refuge and strength. Does the whole earth give way? We say with the psalmist in Psalm 46 that we will not fear. Let the nations rage. Let kingdoms totter. Let economies collapse. Let the waters roar and foam; let the mountains tremble.

Our joy will not be touched, and our hope will not be shaken. In the language of Psalm 46, our God makes wars to cease to the end of the earth. He breaks the bow and shatters the spear. He burns chariots with fire. He fights for us. He fights for justice. He has determined, with all his holy vehemence, that he will be exalted in the earth.

The study of history proves that our times are not uniquely bad. The doctrine of God's sovereignty proves that our efforts are not indispensable to God. The good news of the gospel proves that all the things that matter most to us are not up in the air. The kingdom of God proves that God's will is going to be done on earth as it is in heaven, when heaven and earth become one.

God's power is our peace. His rule is our rejoicing. His help is our hope. His justice is our joy.

Christ has died! Christ is risen! Christ will come again!

Questions for Reflection

1. Why should Christian social engagement be filled with confidence and hope?

2. Spend time reflecting on (or discussing with friends) what the world will one day be. What aspect of the future of God's kingdom is especially encouraging to you?

Chapter 10

Growing Old and Beautiful

God is always faithful to care for his aging saints

I WISH EVERYONE in the world could have met my mom's parents. They are Pop-pop and Nana to me. My Pop-pop is still alive, but Nana passed away during the time I was writing this book. Observing their lives would do more good than reading this chapter or any other chapter on growing old.

A few summers ago, we had a family picnic. Nana's mind was not what it had been because of her growing dementia. Things became so difficult that she didn't remember my name or the fact that I have children. But she had not forgotten the name of her Savior, nor had she forgotten the hymns she spent her life singing.

At that summer picnic, my Pop-pop and Nana sang a few hymns for the rest of us. One of those hymns was "Does Jesus Care?" My dear Nana sang with a smile:

Does Jesus care when my heart is pained
Too deeply for mirth and song;
As the burdens press, and the cares distress
and the way grows weary and long?

Oh, yes, he cares, I know he cares,
His heart is touched with my grief;

99

When the days are weary, the long nights dreary,
I know my Savior cares.

Does Jesus care when I've said goodbye
To the dearest on earth to me,
And my sad heart aches till it nearly breaks—
Is it aught to him? Does he see?

Oh yes he cares . . . I know my Savior cares.[1]

Fortified with a vision of the Savior's care for us, we are empowered to face old age with confidence.

When My Strength Is Spent

What comfort and hope does God give to those who fear the diminishing of our physical, emotional, mental, or spiritual well-being? How can we grow old without bitterness, stubbornness, self-pity, and despair?

Cicero wrote a famous piece of wisdom literature called *How to Grow Old*. One of his observations is that we all want to live into old age, but then we tend to complain when it comes. Growing old is preferable to dying young, but aging is not easy.

Ecclesiastes 12:1–5 gives a poetic description of our aging bodies. What happens when the days of our youth are gone? We will be bent with old age. Strength will fail, teeth will be missing, vision will falter.

In 2 Corinthians 4:16–18, Paul says that we do not lose heart even though our outer self is wasting away. Wasting away means that our health deteriorates, we wake up aching, we get more cavities, we are covered with wrinkles, our bodies sag and creak. Yet in the face of this outward wasting away, we do not lose heart. The reason? "Our inner self is being renewed day by day." And "This light momentary affliction is preparing for us an eternal weight of glory beyond all comparison." In the midst of physical affliction, we regard these hardships as transient and look forward to an unseen and eternal future.

In Psalm 71, a man is contemplating growing old. Verse 9 says, "Do not cast me off in the time of old age; forsake me not when my strength is spent." This is the fear we can experience when we think about growing old. *What if I am alone? What if there is no one to help me in my weakness?* Verse 18 says, "So even to old age and gray hairs, O God, do not forsake me."

The striking thing about Psalm 71 is that we encounter a man who faces aging, but his life is not marked by bitterness, sluggishness, anger, anxiety, and complaining. Rather, his life is marked by joyful resolve:

- In my old age, there will be overwhelming gratitude for past grace. The psalmist remembers that he has leaned upon the Lord from before his birth (v. 6). God has been his hope and his trust from his youth (v. 5), and has been faithful ever since. "O God, from my youth you have taught me, and I still proclaim your wondrous deeds" (v. 17).
- In my old age, there will be joy-filled praise for present grace. "You are my rock and my fortress" (v. 3); "My praise is continually of you" (v. 6). "My mouth is filled with your praise, and with your glory all the day" (v. 8).
- In my old age, there will be vibrant hope in future grace. In verse 14 we hear the psalmist's resolve: "But I will hope continually and will praise you yet more and more." In old age we will proclaim God's might to another generation, and speak of God's power to those who are young (v. 18).

Our strength may be spent, but the strength of our omnipotent God will never be spent. In his power, the weak are made spiritually strong. At his throne of grace, there is mercy and help in time of need. Through the changes and storms of life, the Lord is our eternal shelter.

Deuteronomy 33:25–27 gives a great promise: "As your days, so shall your strength be. There is none like God, O Jeshurun, who rides through the heavens to your help, through the skies in his majesty. The eternal God is your dwelling place, and underneath are the everlasting arms."

My days will not outnumber my strength. My physical strength may fail, but God gives power to the faint. He will renew the strength of my soul, enabling me to mount up with wings like eagles (Isaiah 40:31).

Therefore, I will not be afraid. I will fear no evil. Hope will be my song as I age. Decay, loss, and limitations will only make my hope sing louder by causing me to fix my eyes on the bright future Christ has for me. The only things I can lose are things I didn't deserve in the first place. I will one day gain more than I can possibly lose in this life. And God will empower me by his Spirit to bless his name when loss comes.

What will you say when your strength is failing? In his popular song, "10,000 Reasons," Matt Redman sings of reaching the end of his life, when strength is gone and the day of his departure from this world is at hand. He resolves that on that day, he will still be found singing God's praises. The psalmist says, "Every day I will bless you and praise your name forever and ever" (Psalm 145:2).

Aging with Joy

Many people dread getting old. And certainly old age brings unique challenges and sorrows. Physical weakness and health challenges are reminders that we are moving closer to death and this world is not the way it's supposed to be.

But the accent of Scripture falls not on the sorrows of aging, but on its joys. For the Christian, old age is more about hope than dread, more about honor than dishonor, more about holiness than decay, more about life than death, more about heaven than earth. These are the reasons we age with confidence:

- We have the sure hope that our bodies will be resurrected.
- We know the great honor God bestows on old age.
- We experience the increased holiness God is working in us.
- We have tasted the eternal life that is ours in Christ.
- We long for the rest of heaven that is drawing nearer.

We live in a society that idolizes youth and resists aging. But the Bible takes a much different view. The signs of aging are signs of life. They are visible proof of hard work, valuable activity, and memories made. Every wrinkle, every visible vein, every gray hair is a badge of honor.

Proverbs 16:31 associates old age with glory and godliness: "Gray hair is a crown of glory; it is gained in a righteous life."

Have you ever noticed that elderly people often have a distinct beauty and grace about them? It is a beauty that is far more proven, sacred, and stunning than the beauty of youth. You don't need to try to look twenty years younger than you are.

When the Bible says that someone is "old and full of years" (as it says of Job when he died), it means more than "he was alive a long time." *Full of years* means full of God's favor and blessing.

Mike Mason describes the beauty of elderly saints in lively terms:

Even their physical bodies seem to take on an aura of sanctity. . . .You can see God in the lines of these faces, in the wattles of the neck, in the creases around the eyes and on the mottled hands. These folks are still sinners just like everybody else, and yet one can almost see the sin falling off them. Evil no longer frightens them; they eat it for breakfast. Death does not terrorize; they run swiftly toward it like Olympic youths. . . .

These people are like ancient and unimaginably dangerous gangsters, like Mafia godfathers. Long ago they hung up their sawed-off shotguns, and now their weapons are of an entirely different order; now they transfix you with only their eyes and the gravel in their throats. . . . Their faith has made them untouchable. The blood of Christ has made them incorruptible. Even as they lie on their beds breathing their last, the mighty power of the resurrection is fairly jumping out of their mouths.[2]

By the grace of God, this is the kind of old person you will be.

Have a vision for what flourishing will look like when physical wellness fails you and mental wellness declines. Develop strong convictions that physical weakness and aging will not alter the essence of who you are and what your life is truly about. Thank God for every undeserved breath. Anticipate the harvest of righteousness.

It's true that old age often exacerbates sins that have not been put to death. But old age also multiplies fruit that has been cultivated. And God promises that we will "still bear fruit in old age" (Psalm 92:14).

The reason we can have such confidence is because God will not forsake us. The passage of Scripture that my wife and I chose to have read on our wedding day was Isaiah 46:3–4:

> Listen to me, O house of Jacob,
>   all the remnant of the house of Israel,
> who have been borne by me from before your birth,
>   carried from the womb;
> even to your old age I am he,
>   and to gray hairs I will carry you.
> I have made, and I will bear;
>   I will carry and will save.

When my health is failing, God will not fail me. The one who has carried me from the womb will carry me through whatever old age may bring.

Nothing a Good Resurrection Can't Fix

There a tendency among some Christians to devalue the importance of the body, denigrating the physical and elevating the spiritual. But the gospel speaks a better word.

God has made us to care about the strength and beauty of our bodies. The lesson of aging and weakness is not that a strong, healthy body doesn't matter or that the physical is unimportant. Some Christians are surprised to learn that the gospel is good news for our bodies.

Psalm 103:3 says that one of the Lord's many benefits is that he heals all our diseases. All sickness will one day be gone. In Matthew 8:17, after Jesus heals Peter's mother-in-law and many others, we are told, "This was to fulfill what was spoken by the prophet Isaiah: 'He took our illnesses and bore our diseases.'" Jesus not only bore our guilt and shame, he bore our illnesses and diseases.

This healing, purchased for us through the work of Christ, is not experienced in full until Christ comes again and our bodies are raised to life. But this healing is an essential part of the message of salvation.

The gospel brings the good news of what Christ in his human body has done to secure resurrection, healing, and eternal life for our bodies. The gospel is the story of God-made-flesh taking action for the salvation of the whole person.

In this life, our bodies are weak and ruined in many ways. We know disability, frailty, genetic defects, sickness, and disease. Christ came to make his blessings flow far as the curse is found.

Is your body currently failing you? Do you fear that things will get worse? Look beyond old age, beyond the grave, to the return of Christ and the future of your body. D. A. Carson says, "I'm not suffering from anything that a good resurrection can't fix."[3]

Imagine a body just like your present body, with no health deficiencies, no sickness, no disease, no defects, no fragility, no limping, no pain, no allergies, no aches, no physical or mental impairments. Imagine a body that is recognizable as your own, but more glorious than you can imagine.

Philippians 3:20–21 says, "But our citizenship is in heaven, and from it we await a Savior, the Lord Jesus Christ, *who will transform our lowly body to be like his glorious body*, by the power that enables him even to subject all things to himself" (emphasis added). One day these humble, lowly bodies will be like the glorious, resurrected body of Jesus Christ. What is sick will be healed, what is weak will be strong, what is decaying will be incorruptible.

In Romans 8 we are told, "If the Spirit of him who raised Jesus from the dead dwells in you, he who raised Christ Jesus from the dead will also give life to your mortal bodies through his Spirit who dwells in you" (v. 11). The Spirit of life, who gave you the gift of physical life and then caused you to be born again to new spiritual life, is not yet finished with his life-giving work in you. God, through his Spirit, will give life to your body when Christ returns. Romans 8:23–24 says that this bodily transformation is the great triumph of the gospel and the hope of our salvation: "We ourselves, who have the firstfruits of the Spirit, groan inwardly as we wait eagerly for adoption as sons, the redemption of our bodies. For in this hope we were saved."

First Corinthians 15 is the chapter in all of Scripture that most thoroughly defends, celebrates, and describes this resurrection of the body. Christ has been raised from the dead, in accordance with the Scriptures (v. 4), and he is "the firstfruits of those who have fallen asleep" (v. 20).

> Behold! I tell you a mystery. We shall not all sleep, but we shall all be changed, in a moment, in the twinkling of

an eye, at the last trumpet. For the trumpet will sound, and the dead will be raised imperishable, and we shall be changed. For this perishable body must put on the imperishable, and this mortal body must put on immortality. (1 Corinthians 15:51–53)

The poet Gerard Manley Hopkins compares our spirit dwelling in mortal bodies to a skylark in a dull cage.[4] In these bodies we know drudgery, toil, and aging. Considering the skylark and the human soul, Hopkins says,

> Both sing sometimes the sweetest, sweetest spells,
> Yet both droop deadly sometimes in their cells
> Or wring their barriers in bursts of fear or rage.

However, it's not as if the skylark and the spirit don't need a home. For the skylark, his resting place is found when he flies to his nest, not when he is imprisoned in a cage. Likewise, the great hope of the gospel is not freedom from our bodies, but the resurrection of the flesh and the immortality of the body.

> Man's spirit will be flesh-bound when found at best,
> But uncumbered: meadow-down is not distressed
> For rainbow footing it nor he for his bones risen.

Bones risen! The rising of our bones is our hope and our destiny. Hopkins says that our spirit will not be distressed to be in a risen, glorified body, any more than meadow flowers are distressed to have a rainbow resting on them. This is the future that every aging saint in Christ joyfully awaits.

We Will Prove God's Unchanging Love

None of this means that growing old is easy. But it does mean that we do not experience the grief of aging as those who have no hope.

When I visited my Pop-pop the summer before Nana died, he told me that he never knew he was capable of crying so many tears. He said that the hardest part was not being able to communicate with Nana because of her dementia. They couldn't do games and puzzles like other elderly couples could. We sat on a sofa and he told me, with tears in his eyes, that this isn't the way they had hoped or planned for those years to be. He and I talked a lot about heaven that day.

Through tears I read the beginning of Revelation 21 to my Nana. I could barely finish.

> Then I saw a new heaven and a new earth, for the first heaven and the first earth had passed away, and the sea was no more. And I saw the holy city, new Jerusalem, coming down out of heaven from God, prepared as a bride adorned for her husband. And I heard a loud voice from the throne saying, "Behold, the dwelling place of God is with man. He will dwell with them, and they will be his people, and God himself will be with them as their God. He will wipe away every tear from their eyes, and death shall be no more, neither shall there be mourning, nor crying, nor pain anymore, for the former things have passed away." (Revelation 21:1–4)

That is our future. And until that day, every day of our lives will prove God's unchanging love.

One of my favorite hymns is "How Firm a Foundation." Some modern versions cut the verse on growing old:

> E'en down to old age all My people shall prove
> my sovereign, eternal, unchangeable love;
> and when hoary hairs shall their temples adorn,
> like lambs they shall still in My bosom be borne.[5]

I suppose I can understand why we sometimes remove this verse. (I think it has something to do with singing about "hoary hairs," which simply means hair that is aging and gray.) But I love the truth of this verse, that in our old age we will prove the greatness of God's unchanging love.

What is aging to us? Aging is the accumulation of more stories of the faithfulness of God. It is a visible display of God's determination to love and care for his own.

I have seen saints in my church family age with grace and go on to glory. I saw it in my Nana. By God's grace, old age for you will mean that you know more of Christ. If married, your love for your spouse will grow sweeter still. Your godliness will run deeper. Your influence will grow broader. Your hope will be stronger. The glory of heaven will be closer.

Praise God for his faithfulness to care for his people through old age!

Questions for Reflection

1. Think about someone you know who has aged in a way that honors God and sets an example for others. What do you appreciate and respect about that person?

2. What are some of the joys of aging?

Chapter 11

It Is Not Death to Die

Jesus is our champion, who gives us victory over death

THE THEME OF the last Harry Potter book, *Harry Potter and the Deathly Hallows*, is summarized in a biblical quotation found on the tomb of Harry's parents, James and Lily Potter. The words are from 1 Corinthians 15:26: "The last enemy that shall be destroyed is death."

The book is a powerful resurrection story. The only way for the evil Voldemort to be defeated and for others to be rescued is for Harry (the Chosen One) to sacrifice himself in love, to face death and receive the killing curse. At the climax of the book, Harry walks resolutely to his death as his enemies mock and revile him. He doesn't draw his wand; he doesn't put up a fight. He freely gives himself up.

And it is precisely by giving himself up to death that Harry Potter triumphs and that death is defeated. The story mirrors (as so many do) the eternal truth for which all of humanity longs. The reality of death is unavoidable: we will see loved ones die, and we ourselves will die.

How can we face death with confidence and peace? By knowing the one who removed the sting of death and defeated death for us. Jesus is the Resurrection and the Life. His resurrection secures our own future resurrection. We grieve in the face of death, but we do not grieve as those who have no hope.

When Jesus Comes to the Tomb

In John 11, a large crowd has gathered around the tomb of Lazarus. They thought they came to mourn his death, but God's greater purpose in having them there was to publicly demonstrate the power of Jesus over death.

We read twice that Jesus was "deeply moved" as he came to the tomb (vv. 33, 38). This is not the sorrow we feel when we know we will not see a friend again, nor is it the sorrow of helplessness when we know there is nothing we can do about the situation. Jesus is deeply moved with compassion, yes, but even more, he is deeply moved with outrage.

The Enemy is doing his evil work of ending life, and Jesus is incensed. "Death in the world that I have made? Death taking the ones I love? The victory will not belong to death."

B. B. Warfield, explaining the emotions of Christ in this passage, says, "It is death that is the object of his wrath, and behind death him who has the power of death, and whom he has come into the world to destroy. . . . His soul is held by rage."[1]

Whatever enemies you may have in this world, none compares with death. Nothing is more fearful, more terrible, more ugly. Nothing brings more pain, grief, and confusion into our lives. Death was not originally part of the good world God made; death entered the world as the result of sin.

As Jesus draws near to the tomb of Lazarus, he does not see death as normal. He sees it as an intruder and an impostor, an enemy that brings destruction, separation, and sorrow. When faced with death, Jesus burns with holy rage. He comes to the grave as an angry man who is about to grab death by the jugular.

John Calvin says that Christ approaches the tomb of Lazarus "not . . . as an idle spectator, but as a champion who prepares for a contest; and therefore we need not wonder that he again groans; for the violent tyranny of death, which he had to conquer, is placed before his eyes."[2]

No one in the crowd was expecting anything miraculous to happen. They were as skeptical as you or I would have been. Even Martha, after she had spoken to Jesus, objects to the stone being rolled away: "Lord, by this time there will be an odor" (v. 39). The body had started to decompose. Still, Jesus proceeds. The stone is removed, and the stench of death pours out of the dark cave. The crowd stands by watching, waiting, holding their breath in suspense.

Initially, nothing happens. Everyone looks to Jesus. Jesus addresses his Father: "Thank you that you have heard me. I'm saying this for the sake of all who are listening and watching."

Then, in a loud triumphant cry that could be heard by all, he says, "Lazarus, come forth."

Someone once said that if Jesus hadn't specified *Lazarus*, all the tombs in all the world would have been emptied in that moment.

From inside the tomb of Lazarus, air rushes through a trachea, lungs begin to expand and contract, a heart begins to pound, life-sustaining oxygen spreads through a body once dead.

Satan recoils.

Demons panic in terror.

Angels rejoice.

Death has met its match.

To the shock of everyone present, Lazarus steps from the grave into the sunlight, still wrapped in grave clothes. He is alive by the power of Jesus, who has displayed his victory over sin and death.

The Resurrection and the Life

By raising Lazarus, Jesus was confronting what the Bible calls "the last enemy," which is death. He is pointing forward to his own resurrection which would soon take place, and he is showing that he alone is the way of eternal life.

Jesus lives to calm our troubled hearts. He takes an interest in our sorrows and shares in our grief. He loves us more than we know, and has taken action to secure for us the hope of the resurrection.

When Martha spoke to Jesus about the death of Lazarus, he responded with words of comfort and of hope beyond the grave by drawing attention to himself.

> Jesus said to her, "I am the resurrection and the life. Whoever believes in me, though he die, yet shall he live, and everyone who lives and believes in me shall never die. Do you believe this?" She said to him, "Yes, Lord; I believe that you are the Christ, the Son of God, who is coming into the world." (John 11:25–27)

Jesus wants us to know that because of his resurrection, death does not have the last word. Whoever believes in him—whoever believes in his death for sinners, believes he took the judgment and death we deserve, believes he lives today—whoever believes in him, though he dies physically, yet shall he live. As Jesus says, "Everyone who lives and believes in me shall never die."

Richard Baxter, in his classic book, *The Saints' Everlasting Rest*, says, "The grave that could not keep our Lord cannot keep us. He arose for us, and by the same power will cause us to arise. . . . Let us never look at the grave, but let us see the resurrection beyond it."[3]

For those united to Christ, it is not death to die. Christ Jesus came into the world to destroy all that would destroy us, and defeat anything that would keep us from his love. He is the champion of heaven, who gives us victory over death. He is the resurrection and the life, and through our union with him we too shall rise. The same voice that broke through the tomb of Lazarus will break through our tombs, to the praise of his glory.

How do we know? The death of Christ forever marks the death of death. Octavius Winslow writes,

> Death received a death-wound when Christ died. You face a conquered foe. He stands at your side a crownless king, and waving a broken scepter. Your death shall be another victory over the believer's last foe. Planting your foot of faith upon his prostrate neck, you shall spring into glory, more than a conqueror, through him that loved you.[4]

O Death, Where Is Your Sting?

In 1 Corinthians 15, God says that Jesus through his death and resurrection has removed the sting of death. It's like death is a creature or an insect that has lost its ability to sting.

My wife and I went to the Bahamas to celebrate our tenth wedding anniversary. While we were there, I came across a scorpion in our room. It wasn't a huge thing, but for the purpose of this story, in which I am the hero, let's imagine it was much bigger.

When I first saw the scorpion, it was still. I didn't know if it was alive. I moved the rug it was on, and up went the tail with a stinger on it. I picked up a shoe and declared, "Meghan, stand back."

I didn't know how hard it would be to kill, or how quick it was, so I decided I would unleash on this thing. Around ten hits later, Meghan, who was less impressed with me than I was, said, "That seems a little excessive."

Now, that is essentially what Jesus has done with death. For those who are in Christ, Jesus has beaten down the enemy and death will never sting again.

> "O death, where is your victory? O death, where is your sting?" The sting of death is sin, and the power of sin is

the law. But thanks be to God, who gives us the victory through our Lord Jesus Christ. (1 Corinthians 15:55–57)

Second Corinthians 5 says that our bodily existence in this life is like a tent in which we groan and are burdened, "longing to put on our heavenly dwelling" (v. 2). Presently we are away from the Lord, but when we die, we are with him. "We would rather be away from the body and at home with the Lord" (v. 8). For this reason, in life and in death "we are always of good courage" (v. 6).

In Philippians 1, Paul boldly declares, "To live is Christ, and to die is gain" (v. 21). He loves life and ministry in this world, and yet he says, "My desire is to depart and be with Christ, for that is far better" (v. 23).

At the moment of your death, you enter immediately into a more glorious and joyful existence. You do not need to wait until your resurrection to know the joy of God's presence, even though the resurrection of the body at Christ's return is our ultimate hope. When you die, you will be with Christ, in paradise, and it will be gain.

The pastor and evangelist D. L. Moody once quipped, "Some day you will read in the papers that D. L. Moody, of East North-field, is dead. Don't you believe a word of it! At that moment I shall be more alive than I am now."[5]

Bob Kauflin wrote a song called "It Is Not Death to Die."

It is not death to die
To leave this weary road
And join the saints who dwell on high
Who've found their home with God.
It is not death to close
The eyes long dimmed by tears
And wake in joy before Your throne
Delivered from our fears.[6]

Psalm 116:15 says, "Precious in the sight of the LORD is the death of his saints." And in Revelation 14:13 it says, "Blessed are the dead who die in the Lord from now on."

Joyfully Awaiting Death

In the Old Testament, Job reflects on the fact that death comes to us all. Our days are determined by God, set with limits he has appointed (Job 14:5). Job cries out in his suffering with a question: "If a man dies, shall he live again?" (14:14). Jesus gives a better word than Job's friends when he declares, "Because I live, you also will live" (John 14:19).

Every day we step closer to the grave. As Christians we do not shrink back from that hour, but march toward it as victors and more than conquerors, knowing that death has lost its sting and cannot sever us from the love of Christ. Because Christ lives, we also will live.

Jesus is our brave forerunner. He died as a champion. He declared, "It is finished," and then rose triumphant on the third day. His followers face death with holy courage, knowing that death has been defeated.

- Like Stephen, we will die full of the Holy Spirit, with eyes of faith beholding the glory of the Lord, experiencing the special grace that God gives his dying saints (Acts 7:54–60).
- Like the apostle Paul, we will say with good courage that the time of our departure has come, and we will welcome the finish line to receive the crown of righteousness and the award God has for us (2 Timothy 4:6–8). "I am ready not only to be imprisoned but even to die" (Acts 21:13).
- Like Simeon in the temple, we declare that we will depart in peace (Luke 2:29).

If you are a Christian, you have already been delivered from the fear of death and judgment through the finished work of Christ. Hebrews 2:14–15 says,

> Since therefore the children share in flesh and blood, he himself likewise partook of the same things, that through death he might destroy the one who has the power of death, that is, the devil, and deliver all those who through fear of death were subject to lifelong slavery.

The situation is not so much that I need to overcome the fear of death as it is that I need to know the one who, through his death, overcame the fear of death for me.

You should hate death, but you should not fear it. You should grieve over death, but you should not grieve as those who have no hope. The gospel has removed the sting of death, and has made the ghastly grave a passage to glory and gladness.

Question and Answer 42 of *The Heidelberg Catechism* reminds us of the nature of death for believers. It says, "Our death is not a satisfaction for our sins, but only a dying to sins and entering into eternal life."[7] This is why John Calvin could say, "No one has made progress in the school of Christ who does not joyfully await the day of death and final resurrection."[8] Charles Spurgeon says, "You who are believers in Christ, look forward to death with great joy. Expect it as your springtime of life, the time when your real summer will come and your winter will be over forever."[9]

Farewell Night; Welcome Day

The great preacher Martyn Lloyd-Jones, when he lay on his death bed in his old age, wrote a note for his wife and immediate family on a scrap of paper. It read, "Do not pray for healing. Do not hold me back from the glory."[10]

When John Bradford was in prison, he said, "I have no request to make. If Queen Mary gives me my life, I will thank her;

if she will banish me, I will thank her; if she will burn me, I will thank her; if she will condemn me to perpetual imprisonment, I will thank her."[11]

When Bradford was informed of his impending death, the jailer's wife came running to his chamber in great alarm, telling him that the following day he would be burned. His reply? "Lord, I thank Thee. I have waited for this for a long time. It is not terrible to me. God, make me worthy of such a mercy."[12]

In other words, bring it on.

John Bunyan, at the end of Book 2 of *The Pilgrim's Progress*, describes the ragtag group of pilgrims who are each called home to the Celestial City. Mr. Ready-to-Halt, who had been so ready to stop and give up at every point of the journey, said with his last words, "Welcome life!" and he made it. Mr. Feeble-Mind was called home. Then Mr. Despondency received his letter from the Celestial City, which read, "Trembling man! You are summoned to be ready to meet with the King by the next Lord's Day, and to shout for joy for your deliverance from all your doubtings."

Mr. Despondency's daughter was named Much-Afraid—she had lived her entire life in fears that she was unable to shake. She was called home to her inheritance as well. The last words of Mr. Despondency were, "Farewell night; welcome day." His daughter went through that river singing.

John Bunyan then tells about a Mr. Honest who was also called home. He gathered his friends and said farewell for a time. "The last words of Mr. Honest were . . . 'Grace Reigns!' So he left the world."[13]

Grace reigns. We do not know the time and circumstances surrounding our deaths, but we know they are appointed by the God whose grace forever reigns. His grace will give you peace in the end, in your final moments. When the time comes for us to leave this world, hope will triumph over fear. And in the moment of our dying, earthly sorrows will pass and the joy of Christ's presence will be ours.

In the face of death, we will turn to the word of truth and be made strong. The famous Baptist preacher, F. B. Meyer, in his parting words, said, "Read me something from the Bible, something brave and triumphant."[14]

If I die before my wife, Meghan, this is what I want: *Love, please read me something brave and triumphant.* Maybe 1 Corinthians 15, John 11, John 17, Romans 8, Psalm 23, Psalm 27, or Revelation 21. All of the above, if there's time.

And if Meghan leaves first, and if there is the opportunity, I know I will read her something brave and triumphant. And I know I will need to hear it just as much as she will.

I hate death, but I am ready for it. I believe that I was made for another world—a new world. I believe that in Christ the sting of death has been removed. I believe that the day I die will be better than the day I was born. When you lay me down to die, you lay me down to live. My death will not be a tragedy, and I refuse to grieve as those who have no hope. My God has triumphed over death.

> He will swallow up death forever; and the LORD God will wipe away tears from all faces, and the reproach of his people he will take away from all the earth, for the LORD has spoken. (Isaiah 25:8)

Questions for Reflection

1. What are some of the important truths the Bible teaches about death?

2. What reasons do Christians have to look forward to death?

Chapter 12
Eternal Optimists

True courage comes from knowing the end of the story

HAVE YOU EVER looked at the brokenness of life in this world and wondered what kind of ending the story will have? Will the story have a sorrowful, *Old Yeller* ending? In that film, a boy named Travis loves his dog, Old Yeller. The dog is the boy's best friend. The dog repeatedly saves their lives. The dog becomes infected with rabies while saving the family from an infected wolf. The dog needs to be shot by the boy. *The end.*

That has to be one of the saddest endings ever. Will the story of the world and the story of your life end in sorrow? Or will the story have a confusing ending, like the TV show *Lost*? Never has an ending been so widely anticipated, and never has an ending confused and upset so many people. *You mean I binge-watched half a dozen seasons on Netflix for* **this**?

Will our lives end with a thousand loose ends, as we scratch our heads and wonder, "What was the meaning of *that*?"

No. God is a great author, and the story he is writing ends with a world of joy and victory and life. Heaven will come to earth, the dwelling place of God will be with us, the former things will pass away, and all things will be made new.

The Best Is Yet to Come

Every day we have the comfort of knowing that our best is yet to come. You have a future in Christ that is better than you can imagine. You have a hope that will not disappoint. You will have the life you always wanted.

The *Westminster Larger Catechism* describes your future like this:

> The righteous . . . shall be fully and forever freed from all sin and misery; filled with inconceivable joys, made perfectly holy and happy both in body and soul, in the company of innumerable saints and holy angels, but especially in the immediate vision and fruition of God the Father, of our Lord Jesus Christ, and of the Holy Spirit, to all eternity.[1]

Peter Kreeft, in his book on heaven, says that when we come to understand our future in Christ, it produces the greatest psychological revolution imaginable. Utter fearlessness now marks our lives.

> Now suppose both death and hell were utterly defeated. Suppose the fight was fixed. Suppose God took you on a crystal ball trip into your future and you saw with indubitable certainty that despite everything—your sin, your smallness, your stupidity—you could have free for the asking your whole crazy heart's deepest desire: heaven, eternal joy. Would you not return fearless and singing? What can earth do to you if you are guaranteed heaven? To fear the worst earthly loss would be like a millionaire fearing the loss of a penny—less, a scratch on a penny.[2]

True courage comes from knowing the end of the story.

A Vision of the Future

The churches in Revelation are in many ways like our churches today. We are often fearful and troubled, we face tribulation and slander, we are plagued by our own sins, and we have but little power. We know tears and sickness and death.

Like those churches, we too must hear the words of our Savior triumphantly declaring the bright tomorrow that is coming soon. Nothing but a clear vision of our future will remove fear and strengthen our souls.

The book of Revelation is a "revelation of Jesus Christ" (1:1), given to John as he was on the island of Patmos in order to show the people of Christ "the things that must soon take place" (1:1). Jesus Christ is introduced as "the faithful witness, the firstborn of the dead, and the ruler of the kings on earth" (1:5). As faithful witness, he testifies to the truth. As the firstborn of the dead, he is the resurrected forerunner who rose from death that we too might rise in him. As the ruler of the kings on earth, he is the sovereign Lord of history, the Alpha and the Omega, the Almighty.

This same Jesus is the one who commanded these things to be written, that we might know the things that will take place in the future. He reminds us of the coming Tree of Life from which we will eat, our victory over the second death that has been secured by his substitutionary death, the authority we will have over the nations as we sit with Christ on his throne, and the new name we will receive that will be confessed by Christ before the Father and his angels and forever written in the Book of Life.

Jesus has conquered, and through our union with him, we are more than conquerors. He says, "The one who conquers, I will grant him to sit with me on my throne, as I also conquered and sat down with my Father on his throne" (Revelation 3:21). It is from this throne that John hears a loud voice declaring,

> Behold, the dwelling place of God is with man. He will dwell with them, and they will be his people, and God himself will be with them as their God. He will wipe away every tear from their eyes, and death shall be no

> more, neither shall there be mourning, nor crying, nor
> pain anymore, for the former things have passed away.
> And he who was seated on the throne said, "Behold, I am
> making all things new." (Revelation 21:3–5)

So much of our present, daily experience in this world is described
in the words of this passage.

Mourning. Crying. Pain. Death. What we celebrate in the
gospel of the resurrection of Jesus Christ is the great truth that
because Jesus lives, these realities are not the end of the story.
Christians are eternal optimists, because we know how the story
ends. Jesus triumphs, and we along with him.

All Things New

The promise of Jesus to make all things new is a reminder of the
cosmic scope of redemption. Romans 8:22 says that "the whole
creation has been groaning together in the pains of childbirth
until now." We hear the creation groaning every day.

But louder than creation's groaning is the music of hope that
sounds forth in the gospel. The message of redemption includes
the good news that God has not abandoned the world he made,
but has sent his Son, who through his death and resurrection
would save sinners and make all things new.

Michael Reeves said that the tomb from which Christ
emerged became the womb of a new creation.[3] The resurrection
of Christ is the inauguration of the new creation.

At present, there is only one physical reality that has been
fully renewed, and that is the body of Jesus Christ. But when he
comes again, all of his people, along with the physical world in
which we live, will be renewed.

"The Lord does not forsake the work of his hands," writes Al
Wolters. "In faithfulness he upholds his creation order. Even the
great crisis that will come on the world at Christ's return will not
annihilate God's creation or our cultural development of it. The

new heaven and the new earth the Lord has promised will be a continuation, purified by fire, of the creation we now know."[4]

In C. S. Lewis's *The Lion, the Witch, and the Wardrobe*, Mr. Beaver recites a famous rhyme in Narnia, speaking of a time to come.

> "Wrong will be right, when Aslan comes in sight,
> At the sound of his roar, sorrows will be no more,
> When he bares his teeth, winter meets its death,
> And when he shakes his mane, we shall have spring
>   again."[5]

We too have received an ancient prophecy, the promise of a new heavens and a new earth. Every wrong will be put right, sorrows will be no more, winter will meet its death. God spoke through the prophet Isaiah, declaring,

> "For behold, I create new heavens and a new earth, and the former things shall not be remembered or come into mind. But be glad and rejoice forever in that which I create; for behold, I create Jerusalem to be a joy, and her people to be a gladness. I will rejoice in Jerusalem and be glad in my people; no more shall be heard in it the sound of weeping and the cry of distress." (Isaiah 65:17–19)

This is the new heavens and the new earth. The former things will give way to a world of indescribable joy and gladness. No weeping. No distress. No hunger, no thirst, no oppressive heat (Revelation 7:16).

Words fail to describe what that world will be! We will be free from everything sin and the curse have brought into the world. Your heart will understand far more deeply than ever before just how much the Father loves you, and you will realize just how homesick you've been. You will be glad and rejoice forever in the world God creates.

Remember that the Christian hope is not consummated when we die, but when Christ comes again. We do not look forward primarily to death and the intermediate state, but to the return of Christ, the resurrection of the body, and the renewal of all creation.

It cannot be emphasized strongly enough that our future is material and bodily, affirming the goodness of the created world. A salvation that renews the soul but not the body is not a full salvation. A salvation that renews the individual but not the created world is not a full salvation.

Redemption doesn't mean that the created world doesn't matter; redemption means that the created world is a part of God's purpose and will be renewed in Christ. Heaven is coming soon to the earth in which we dwell. All will be renewed and transformed. The paradise once lost will be regained with surpassing glory. And it will be glorious beyond all imagining.

To Enjoy God Forever

What makes our future so glorious, and what makes the new heavens and the new earth so satisfying, is that we will enjoy the presence of God and praise him forever. The psalmist says to the Lord, "Whom have I in heaven but you? And there is nothing on earth that I desire besides you" (Psalm 73:25). The greatest blessing of heaven is the presence of God, without which heaven ceases to be heaven.

The final chapter of Scripture, Revelation 22, describes the river of the water of life, bright as crystal, that flows from the throne of God and of the Lamb.

> No longer will there be anything accursed, but the throne of God and of the Lamb will be in it, and his servants will worship him. They will see his face, and his name will be on their foreheads. And night will be no more. They will need no light of lamp or sun, for the Lord God will be

their light, and they will reign forever and ever. (Revelation 22:3–5)

Cornelis Venema observes, "When the Bible speaks of the believer's future, it is this enjoyment of God, this 'seeing God face to face' that is most emphasized."[6]

This deeper knowledge of God includes a greater enjoyment of him and a fuller trust in him. Richard Baxter says that in heaven, we will rest from all our doubts of God's love. He observes that our experience in this life involves "sometimes cruel thoughts of God, sometimes undervaluing thoughts of Christ, sometimes unbelieving thoughts of Scripture, sometimes injurious thoughts of Providence."[7] But in heaven, these things will be no more.

First Thessalonians 4 describes what will happen when Christ returns, for the strengthening of our hope and the encouragement of our souls. The voice of the archangel will be lifted in triumph, the trumpet of God will sound, and the Lord Jesus Christ himself will descend from heaven (v. 16). That is when all of God's people, whether dead or alive, will meet Christ together in the skies. That is when all God's people will be glorified. While our conversions came at different times, glorification will come at the same time for us all. Most astoundingly, "we will always be with the Lord" (v. 17).

There is a reason Revelation 5 describes the Lamb standing, as though it had been slain, as the focus of heaven's praise. His presence will be our joy and our peace forever. One hymn says,

> The Bride eyes not her garment,
> But her dear Bridegroom's face;
> I will not gaze at glory
> But on my King of grace;
> Not at the crown He giveth
> But on His pierced hand:
> The Lamb is all the glory
> Of Immanuel's land.[8]

On the Brink of Eternity

The goal throughout this book has been to cultivate confidence as we look to the future. Fearful thoughts of the future can be replaced by the Spirit with the glorious inheritance we have in Christ. We can laugh at the times to come, knowing the goodness of the Lord in his faithfulness and his promises.

In the long run, what is the worst-case scenario for our lives?

- If greater sickness and pain are ahead, in a little while we will be perfectly healed. A new body will be ours in the resurrection, full of strength and glory.
- If we enter into days of loneliness, soon we will be together in the great gathering of all God's people, reuniting with loved ones in Christ and enjoying fellowship with the Father, Son, and Holy Spirit forever.
- If loss is ahead, we will later come to know an inheritance that far surpasses all we have parted with in this life. We are fellow heirs with Christ (Romans 8:17), who is himself heir of all things (Hebrews 1:2), which means, incredibly, that all things are yours—"the world or life or death or the present or the future—all are yours" (1 Corinthians 3:21–22).
- If we come to know overwhelming sorrows, eternal gladness and ever-increasing joy come with the bright tomorrow.
- If death comes sooner than we thought, we will be with Christ, which is far better, and we will understand more of the perfect ways of the Lord than we presently do, and we will one day rise in victory over death, dwelling in a world in which death is no more.

We know that difficulties are ahead, and yet we will be confident. Charles Spurgeon says,

The Christian can stand serenely on the brink of eternity and say, 'Come on! Let every event foretold become a fact! Pour out your vials, you angels! Fall, you star called Wormwood! Come, Gog and Magog, to the last great battle of Armageddon!' Nothing is to be feared by those who are one with Jesus. To us remains nothing but joy and rejoicing.[9]

Nothing is to be feared by those who are one with Jesus. That is the Christian position. You stand on the brink of eternity and say, "Come on! Come at me! Christ is with me, and he is greater than my fears."

The antichrists of false messiahs and false prophets cannot harm us. Wars and earthquakes and famine can never steal our hope. Let the dragon and the beast of the sea do their best. Let hail and fire fall; let Babylon rage. Let the earth give way and the mountains be moved into the heart of the sea, let the mountains tremble. God is with us! God will never leave us! And by God's grace we will be faithful to Christ and his gospel, come what may.

We are willing and ready to suffer. We will conquer and overcome. We go bravely into the battle of Armageddon, knowing the God of peace will crush Satan under our feet (Romans 16:20).

The Promise-Keeper has spoken. His grace and goodness will follow us. Fear and anxiety are behind us. The glory of heaven is in our eyes. The kingdom will be consummated. Death will be defeated. Eternal comfort and good hope belong to us by grace.

Come, Lord Jesus

This biblical vision of the future is what we call to mind in times of weakness and fear. In Christ, we know the end of the story. The one "who loves us and has freed us from our sins by his blood" (Revelation 1:5) is the same one "who is coming with the clouds, and every eye will see him" (Revelation 1:6). Soon we will look on the King of grace. The Lamb who was slain for us is making all things new.

I cannot see everything that lies ahead. But I can hear the mountains and the hills singing. I can hear the trees clapping their hands. I can smell a feast of rich food and well-aged wine. I see joy in the morning.

Come, marriage supper of the Lamb! Come, perfect holiness! Come, rich fellowship with all the saints of God in a world of love! Come, unbreakable communion with God for all eternity! Come, Lord Jesus!

God has revealed a bright tomorrow. As we await the Lord's return, may indestructible hope reign in our hearts. May we look to the future without fear. And through days of joy and days of sorrow, may the Lord empower us to know that all will be well.

Questions for Reflection

1. How does the book of Revelation help Christians who are weak and troubled?

2. Read Revelation 21:1–7. What are some of the "former things" that will pass away when Christ returns, and what is our ultimate hope?

Acknowledgments

THIS BOOK WOULD not be possible without Barbara Juliani and the talented team at New Growth Press. In addition to providing the opportunity to publish, working with them is a joy. I am especially grateful to Sue Lutz for her editorial labors.

Covenant Fellowship Church is family to me, and I thank God for each one of the members. My pastors and many others in the church have cared for me and my family over the past two years, and they have done so with much prayer and affection.

My wife and kids are my favorite people in the world. Meghan helps me get through life, supporting and encouraging me in countless ways. She is my best friend and the only girl I have ever fallen in love with. I am grateful for my children, Ryle, Ben, Lily, Isaac, Juliet, and Agatha. They make the home a place of joy, richness, and adventure. I love and enjoy each one of them.

Notes

Chapter 1

1. D. Martyn Lloyd-Jones, *Spiritual Depression: Its Causes and Its Cure* (Grand Rapids, MI: Eerdmans, 1965), 97.

2. Raymond C. Ortlund Jr., *Supernatural Living for Natural People: The Life-Giving Message of Romans 8* (Fearn, Ross-Shire: Christian Focus Publications, 2001), 135.

3. Randy Alcorn, *We Shall See God: Charles Spurgeon's Classic Devotional Thoughts on Heaven* (Carol Stream, IL: Tyndale House Publishers, 2011), 159.

4. Mary Bowley Peters, "All Will Be Well" (1847).

5. Cornelis P. Venema, *The Promise of the Future* (Edinburgh: The Banner of Truth Trust, 2000), 11.

6. Charles Spurgeon, *Beside Still Waters: Words of Comfort for the Soul*, ed. Roy H. Clarke (Nashville, TN: Thomas Nelson, Inc., 1999), 120.

Chapter 2

1. John Stott, *The Cross of Christ* (Downers Grove, IL: InterVarsity Press, 1986), 159.

2. Quoted by David Calhoun in *Suffering and the Goodness of God*, ed. Morgan and Peterson (Wheaton, IL: Crossway Books, 2008), 199–200.

3. John Flavel, *Triumphing Over Sinful Fear* (Grand Rapids, MI: Reformation Heritage Books, 2011), 29.

Chapter 3

1. Charles Spurgeon, *Beside Still Waters*, 12.

2. John Piper, *Future Grace* (Colorado Springs, CO: Multnomah Books, 1995), 65.

3. John Bunyan, *The Pilgrim's Progress* (Wheaton, IL: Crossway, 2009), 66.

4. J. C. Ryle, *Expository Thoughts on the Gospels: Matthew* (Carlisle, PA: The Banner of Truth Trust, 1986), 61.

5. Charles Spurgeon, *Beside Still Waters*, 178.

Chapter 4

1. Martin Luther King Jr., "Shattered Dreams"; http://www.the kingcenter.org/archive/document/shattered-dreams.

2. Herman Bavinck, *Reformed Dogmatics, Volume Four: Holy Spirit, Church, and New Creation* (Grand Rapids, MI: Baker Academic, 2008), 49–50.

3. Jeremiah Burroughs, *Hope* (Orlando, FL: Soli Deo Gloria Publications, 2005), 2.

4. William Gurnall, *The Christian in Complete Armour, Volume 3* (East Peoria, IL: Versa Press, 1989), 174.

5. Ibid., 177.

6. Timothy Keller, *Making Sense of God: An Invitation to the Skeptical* (New York, NY: Viking, 2016), 173.

7. Todd Billings, *Rejoicing in Lament: Wrestling with Incurable Cancer & Life in Christ* (Grand Rapids, MI: Brazos Press, 2015), 89.

8. Kelly Kapic, *Embodied Hope: A Theological Meditation on Pain and Suffering* (Downers Grove, IL: IVP Academic), 33.

9. John Owen, *The Grace and Duty of Being Spiritually Minded, from The Works of John Owen, Volume 7* (Carlisle, PA: Banner of Truth, 1965), 322.

Chapter 5

1. Joni Eareckson Tada, Joni and Friends Radio, September 18, 2015; http://www.joniandfriends.org/radio/5-minute/defiant-joy/.

2. Quoted in Randy Alcorn, *We Shall See God: Charles Spurgeon's Classic Devotional Thoughts on Heaven*, 237–38.

3. http://christianfunnypictures.com/2012/04/peanuts-comic-and-sound-theology.html

4. John Calvin, Commentary on Zechariah 8:15; www.sacred-texts.com/chr/calvin/cc30/cc30011.htm.

5. John Calvin, Commentary on Joshua 10:8; www.sacred-texts.com/chr/calvin/cc07/cc07012.htm.

6. William Gurnall, *The Christian in Complete Armour, Volume 3*, 160.

7. Quoted in J. I. Packer, *Knowing God* (Downers Grove: IL, InterVarsity Press, 1973), 115.

8. John Flavel, *Triumphing Over Sinful Fear* (Grand Rapids, MI: Reformation Heritage Books, 2011), 59.

Chapter 6

1. Marcus Peter Johnson, *One with Christ: An Evangelical Theology of Salvation* (Wheaton IL: Crossway, 2013), 174.

2. Sam Storms, *Kept for Jesus: What the New Testament Really Teaches about Assurance of Salvation and Eternal Security* (Wheaton, IL: Crossway, 2015), 24.

3. Greg Forster, *The Joy of Calvinism: Knowing God's Personal, Unconditional, Irresistible, Unbreakable Love* (Wheaton, IL: Crossway, 2012), 130.

4. John Bunyan, *The Pilgrim's Progress*, 52.

5. J. I. Packer, *Knowing God* (Downers Grove, IL: InterVarsity Press, 1993), 275.

6. Ibid., 270.

7. C. H. Spurgeon, "Good Cheer for Many That Fear," Sermon No. 2815; https://www.ccel.org/ccel/spurgeon/sermons49.iv.html.

8. Octavius Winslow, *No Condemnation in Christ Jesus: As Unfolded in the Eighth Chapter of the Epistle to the Romans* (Edinburgh: The Banner of Truth Trust, 1991), 385.

Chapter 7

1. William Cowper, "God Moves in a Mysterious Way" (1774).

2. David Powlison, *Breaking the Addictive Cycle: Deadly Obsessions or Simple Pleasures?* (Greensboro, NC: New Growth Press, 2010), 8.

3. *The Heidelberg Catechism*, Question and Answer 1, from *Ecumenical Creeds and Reformed Confessions* (Grand Rapids, IL: Faith Alive, 2001).

4. John Calvin, *Institutes of The Christian Religion*, 1.17.3.

5. John Calvin, *Institutes of The Christian Religion*, 1.16.3.

6. Calvin, Commentary of Joshua 6; www.ccel.org/ccel/calvin/calcom07.ix.i.html.

7. Charles Spurgeon, *Beside Still Waters: Words of Comfort for the Soul*, 169.

8. John Stott, *The Cross of Christ* (Downers Grove, IL: InterVarsity Press, 1986), 329.

Chapter 8

1. Leif Enger, *Peace Like a River* (New York, NY: Grove Press, 2001), 36.

Chapter 9

1. See John Perkins, *Let Justice Roll Down* (Grand Rapids, MI: Baker Books, 2014).

2. Russell Moore, *Onward: Engaging Culture without Losing the Gospel* (Nashville, TN: B&H Publishing Group, 2015), 66.

3. Ibid., 97–98.

4. Gary Haugen, *Good News about Injustice: A Witness of Courage in a Hurting World* (Downers Grove, IL: InterVarsity Press, 1999), 61.

5. Ibid., 67.

6. Carl Henry, quoted by Tim Challies on August 30, 2014; https://www.challies.com/a-la-carte/weekend-a-la-carte-august-30/.

7. Kevin DeYoung, *The Hole in Our Holiness: Filling the Gap between Gospel Passion and the Pursuit of Godliness* (Wheaton, IL: Crossway, 2012), 21.

8. Russell Moore, *Onward: Engaging Culture without Losing the Gospel*, 66–67.

9. Andrew Peterson, *The Monster in the Hollows* (Nashville, TN: Rabbit Room Press , 2011), 281.

10. Charles Spurgeon, *Beside Still Waters: Words of Comfort for the Soul*, 169.

11. John M. Perkins, *Let Justice Roll Down* (Grand Rapids, MI: Baker Books, 1976), 11.

12. Quoted by David B. Calhoun, "The Hope of Heaven," in *Heaven* (Wheaton, IL: Crossway, 2014), 261.

Chapter 10

1. Frank E. Graeff, "Does Jesus Care?" (1901).

2. Mike Mason, *The Gospel According to Job* (Wheaton, IL: Crossway, 1994), 445–46.

3. D. A. Carson, quoted on Twitter, @dacarsonspeaks on September 8, 2016.

4. Gerard Manley Hopkins, "The Caged Skylark," *Selected Poems of Gerard Manley Hopkins* (Mineola, NY: Dover Publications, Inc.), 26.

5. Hymn lyrics attributed to Robert Keene, "How Firm a Foundation" (1787).

Chapter 11

1. B. B. Warfield, *The Emotional Life of Our Lord*, from *The Person and Work of Christ* (Phillipsburg, NJ: The Presbyterian and Reformed Publishing Company, 1950), 117.

2. John Calvin, Commentary on John 11; www.ccel.org/study/John_11:38-44.

3. Richard Baxter, *The Saints' Everlasting Rest, from The Practical Works of The Rev. Richard Baxter, Vol. 22* (London: Mills, Jowett, and Mills, 1830), 82–83.

4. Octavius Winslow, *No Condemnation in Christ Jesus: As Unfolded in the Eighth Chapter of the Epistle to the Romans* (Edinburgh: The Banner of Truth Trust, 1991), 385.

5. D. L. Moody, quoted by William R. Moody in *The Life of Dwight L. Moody*, 1900; http://www.ntslibrary.com/PDF%20Books/Life%20of%20Moody.pdf.

6. Bob Kauflin, "It Is Not Death to Die" (2008). Used by permission.

7. *The Heidelberg Catechism*, Question and Answer 42, from *Ecumenical Creeds and Reformed Confessions* (Grand Rapids, MI: Faith Alive, 2001).

8. John Calvin, *Institutes*, 3.9.5.

9. Charles Spurgeon, *Beside Still Waters: Words of Comfort for the Soul*, 128.

10. Iain H. Murray, *D. Martyn Lloyd-Jones: The Fight of Faith 1939-1981* (Carlisle, PA: Banner of Truth, 1990), 747.

11. Quoted in J. C. Ryle, *Holiness: Its Nature, Hindrances, Difficulties, and Roots* (Darlington: Evangelical Press, 1979), 121.

12. Quoted in John Flavel, *Triumphing Over Sinful Fear* (Grand Rapids, MI: Reformation Heritage Books, 2011), 38.

13. John Bunyan, *The Pilgrim's Progress*, 424–26. Quotes lightly edited for modernization.

14. Herbert Lockyer, *Last Words of Saints and Sinners: 700 Final Quotes from the Famous, the Infamous, and the Inspiring Figures of History* (Grand Rapids, MI: Kregel Publications, 1969), 72–73.

Chapter 12

1. *Westminster Larger Catechism*, Question 90.

2. Peter Kreeft, *Heaven: The Heart's Deepest Longing* (San Francisco, CA: Ignatius Press, 1989), 183.

3. Michael Reeves, *Rejoicing in Christ* (Downers Grove, IL: IVP Academic, 2015), 64.

4. Al Wolters, *Creation Regained: Biblical Basics for a Reformational Worldview*, Second edition (Grand Rapids, MI: Wm. B. Eerdmans Publishing Co., 2005), 46–47.

5. C. S. Lewis, *The Lion, the Witch, and the Wardrobe* (New York, NY: HarperCollins, 1950), 85.

6. Cornelis Venema, *The Promise of the Future* (Edinburgh: The Banner of Truth Trust, 2000), 483.

7. Richard Baxter, *The Saints' Everlasting Rest*, from *The Practical Works of The Rev. Richard Baxter, Vol. 22* (London: Mills, Jowett, and Mills, 1830), 145.

8. Anne R. Cousin, "The Sands of Time Are Sinking" (1857).

9. Quoted in Randy Alcorn, *We Shall See God: Charles Spurgeon's Classic Devotional Thoughts on Heaven* (Carol Stream, IL: Tyndale House Publishers, 2011), 158.